I awoke one morning extremely excited-as only a nine-year-old can. Today was the day. This trip had been in the planning stages for weeks; an automobile trip to Indiana. This may not sound out of the ordinary today; however, in the late 1930's automobiles were not as commonplace as today, especially in New York City. My excitement was short lived when I realized I did not feel good. I dreaded telling my mother; she had one solution for all discomfort, Enemas! As the day progressed, I was experiencing a definite pain in my side. When the doctor arrived, after his office hours, he found me doubled over in pain, and rushed me to the hospital. My temperature soared to an unheard of 108 degrees, and after doing everything they could the doctors took my parents aside and told them it was just a matter of time.

What happened to reverse that declaration? The answer to that and many other questions lie within these pages. However, I will report that as a result of that experience, I can state emphatically - miracles happen!

Rev Joanne Dator is an inspirational teacher, speaker and author. A lifetime of personal spiritual discovery only reinforces for me just how powerful Rev Joanne Dator's belief is in the Truth Principles she expresses. We can all benefit tremendously as individuals from this dynamic work that is highly applicable to the betterment of our lives. I find this to be an extraordinary set of life lessons, an invaluable contribution to one's library, and something to be referred to time and time again.

Rev Marlene Davis

Rev. Joanne Dator inspires me with her Truth messages. She is gifted with the ability to present New Thought messages with timeless applications of Jesus' teachings. I was especially moved by her own life story and how she related her own spiritual journey to her Sunday talks. Joanne has a strong consciousness that leaves me enlightened each time I encounter her. I appreciate her love and wisdom and I know that her readers will reach the same conclusion.

John Meeks, Teacher,
Board President of Unity Church

I have studied with many different teachers throughout my 'spiritual road of enlightenment' and I must say that Rev. Joanne Dator has been one of the greatest teachers I've encountered. This book represents many of the inspiring lessons of life that can be enjoyed by all people. Rev. Dator has applied her strong sense of integrity and knowledge that is found within the pages of this book. I strongly feel that any individual who is 'seeking' a spiritual path will find the answers they seek if they 'listen' to what they read in these pages. I personally thank you Rev. Dator for being a great light of God-love in expression.

Kit Barrilleaux,
Unity Student

"Reflections In Light" is a collection of inspirational lessons and messages given by Rev. Dator in her years as an ordained Unity minister. She explains complex spiritual principles and concepts in an easy to understand and matter of fact manner while never talking down to her audience. Rev. Dator tackles subjects as complex as the book of Revelation and as instructional as the origin of the Unity movement by Charles and Myrtle Fillmore. She uses stories and humor to illustrate the New Thought truths to which she has dedicated her career. After reading this inspirational collection, I will never think of the "Three Little Pigs" in the same way again! This is a book that should be on the "must read" list of every seeker of spiritual truth.

Rev. Linda M. Moore

Reverend Joanne Dator is one of the most inspirational Unity ministers I have ever had the pleasure of hearing. She touches the very soul of Unity Principles, clearly, concisely and in a manner that makes you not only understand, but also feel within your very being that you are one with Your Christ within. Her Sunday lectures as well as the classes she teaches have helped me personally to realize how easy and wonderful life can be if you only let it.

Yvonne Starr,
Unity Student

AuthorHouse™
1663 Liberty Drive, Suite 200
Bloomington, IN 47403
www.authorhouse.com
Phone: 1-800-839-8640

© 2008 Joanne M. Dator. All rights reserved.

No part of this book may be reproduced, stored in a retrieval system, or transmitted by any means without the written permission of the author.

First published by AuthorHouse 11/25/2008

ISBN: 978-1-4389-2016-0 (sc)

Library of Congress Control Number: 2008909112

Printed in the United States of America
Bloomington, Indiana

This book is printed on acid-free paper.

Reflections in Light

Joanne M. Dator

I dedicate this book to my first teacher, Doris Standish and to the many beautiful souls which followed after. The names are many. Some have passed but their memory and gifts will remain. They were my teachers and fellow students at Unity Village in the seventies. Next, the blessed group who believed in the teachings and in me, with their help and support together we began the foundation of Christ Unity Church of Panama City Florida, which thrives today. To the many congregants who urged me to write down my messages thank you for planting the seed in my consciousness. I wish to express my love and gratitude to my children who supported me in my choice of becoming a Unity minister. Last but far from least, I dedicate this book to those who are seeking answers to the meaning of life; may you find some solace in your inquiry.

        God Bless You All,
        * Numaskar,
        Rev. Joanne M. Dator
        * I behold The Christ in you.

CONTENTS

Introduction	1
Prologue	3
PART ONE	**7**
Chapter I: Ask, and You Shall Receive	9
Chapter II: Heart's Desire	13
Chapter III: Proof of God at Work	19
Chapter IV: What Is New Thought?	27
Chapter V: The Unity Movement (part 2)	33
Chapter VI: The Unity Movement (part 3)	37
Chapter VII: Before They Call	41
Chapter VIII: The Eleventh Hour	45
Chapter IX: Prayer and Meditation	49
PART TWO	**57**
Chapter X: The Twelve Powers	59
Chapter XI: Strength	65
Chapter XII: Your Inherent Judgment	71
Chapter XIII: Love Is a Power	77
Chapter XIV: Imagination Is a Gift	83
Chapter XV: Wherein Lies the Power	91
Chapter XVI: Understanding	97
Chapter XVII: Will	103
Chapter XVIII: Divine Order	109
Chapter XIX: The Importance of Zeal	115
Chapter XX: Renunciation/Elimination	121
Chapter XXI: Life	127
PART THREE	**133**
Chapter XXII: Holidays	135
Chapter XXIII: Enter His Gates with Thanksgiving	137
Chapter XXIV: God, Man, Santa Claus	143
Chapter XXV: John before Jesus	149
Chapter XXVI: The Virgin Birth	155
Chapter XXVII: Enter Jerusalem	161
Chapter XXVIII: Christ is Risen	167
Addendum	173
Epilogue	181

INTRODUCTION

In our modern society, we have become a people who fear their neighbors, even members of their own families. Muggings, abductions, and murder, which began with Cain and Abel, have been a part of that fear. Because of the annihilation of the World Trade Center on 9/11, the fear of terrorism has escalated to our shore bringing with it a sense of despondency. We have become greedy in the race to stockpile more things and make more money; as a result have isolated ourselves from each other. We have even gone so far as to neglect our children. Our forefathers founded this government on religious freedom. Today a faction would like to see God taken out of that equation. There is a saying that it takes only one rotten apple to spoil the barrel. It is my desire, with knowledge and introspection, to pluck that one apple out of the barrel and to remind people that respect and responsibility should be spontaneous.

It is my wish that in reading this book your awareness will quicken and you will once again believe that Life is Good, that in reality each of us has control of our lives, and change is possible. Most of all I long to instill confidence and viability in the Higher Power, or whatever name you choose to give it, that created us.

> God is no respecter of persons. He doesn't create prophets, seers, sages, and saviors as such. He creates men. But here and there one recognizes his true identity, recognizes the oneness of his life with the Source whence it came. He lives in the realization of this oneness, and in turn becomes a prophet, seer, sage, or savior."
>
> -Ralph Waldo Trine

PROLOGUE

Being an only child, I was an avid reader and books were my companions more often than other children. In my adult life, it never occurred to me to write a book. In fact, if anyone had suggested it in my early years, I would have laughed aloud at such a ludicrous idea. I am retired now. At every stage of our lives we come to a fork in the road where we make new decisions, and explore different pathways. At this stage of my life, I decided to try my hand at becoming an author.

This little book contains not only meaningful events that have happened to me, but also my ministerial messages. These talks given over many years include some personal references, facts, and scriptures from the King James Bible. The messages written exactly as given on a Sunday morning service, and therefore may contain some points repeated for emphasis. May you discover the ideas interesting and thought provoking.

As with all young girls of my generation, my youth consisted of school, work, and then marriage. I was content in the early years, busy running a home and raising our three children. Although I was in awe of God and had faith in Him, I was not a devout churchgoer. If anyone had predicted that I would become an ordained minister, I would have said he or she was crazy. When I take the time to look back on my life I realize what a miracle it was/is, how God, the Universe, a Higher Power, guided me to my destiny.

My introduction into Unity occurred in different stages. Once there, I knew I was home and my intense desire was to teach the Truth of Unity, not as a religion, per se, but as a <u>Spiritual</u> way of life. Let me assure you, dear reader, I am not writing this book to change anyone's views. It is my way to give back some of what I have learned and taught. If it resonates with you, fine; if it gets you thinking, great; if not, that is fine too. It is your right, as God's child, to choose and follow your own beliefs.

Within this little book are the messages I delivered from the pulpit. Over the years, those in the congregation would approach me and ask, "Have you ever thought of writing a book?" I would hear those words and wonder to myself, "Who? Me?" That thought never crossed my mind. I could write a Sunday message, and compose class work that took me days of heavy perspiration and nerve-wracking research, but a book! However, people continued to ask me the question and I began to think the universe was conspiring against me. The straw that broke this "camel's back" occurred when I attended a church auction and purchased an astrology reading. During the reading, (yes, you guessed it,) the astrologer said, "Have you ever thought of writing a book?" Hesitantly, I told her no even though many urged me to put my messages in one. The astrologer firmly stated that I should do it and do it now.

In all fairness, I must admit several months before the reading I attended a writer's group at my church. I felt a bit out of place. The stories read aloud which were done for homework, sounded very 'experienced' to me. Then the leader of the group gave us an assignment. She passed around several gems and asked us to pick one and write a story around it. We had a fifteen-minute limit. I shrank in my chair. I did not think I would be able to come up with anything right off the top of my head. I sat there staring at the pad and pencil in hand while the others furiously attacked the assignment. After using up half of my time, I started writing:

The Crystal Speaks

The purity of being and the clouded side of being; I appear as two but in fact am one. The clouded side allows the light to penetrate which gives hope to all who see me. I am cool to the touch, which calms the heat of negative emotions. Gazing on the pure side brings clarity and a desire to see more of life. The many exterior sides of me open up to the many ways one can view life and its beautiful promises. The deeper one looks into me images appear that testify to a deeper knowing within. I am one with nature as you are. I grow at a slow rate of speed as you do. Within the depth of my being lie promises which lie within you also. We are one! We are eternal! We are indestructible!

I closed my pad, put my pen away and breathed a sigh of relief. After we each took turns reading our work, I heard the words, "For our next exercise," and I wanted to get up and run. I must admit they were very kind about my first attempt, but I was not sure how my luck would hold up. When I heard the assignment, I knew I was doomed. We were to write about something that happened repeatedly on the same day of the week. Suddenly my mind cleared, a smile appeared on my face and I began.

THE PHONE CALL

It is Monday morning, and I wait expectantly for his call. He is thoughtful, kind, and loving. Our relationship grows deeper as the years fly by. The distance between us does not seem so vast when I can hear his voice. He wants to know about my weekend, the activities I participated in, how church went, whom did I see and speak to. His interest is gratifying. Is it possible to feel so much love for one man? The phone rings, I answer eagerly as he says, "Hello, Mom?"

There you have it-the extent of my literary pursuits. Granted, as I said earlier, over the past three decades, I have written many messages for Sunday morning service; however, I did not consider that writing. They were lessons derived from researching other authors, metaphysical texts, and the Bible, but who am I to question fate? I firmly believe that if we, as Jesus said *"have ears to hear,"* then everyone and everything is a messenger from God. There have been too many such messengers urging me to do this.

It is my sincere wish you enjoy the book. Most of all, I trust that it will pique some interest, and some awareness of your own messengers.

PART ONE

CHAPTER I:
Ask, and You Shall Receive

Good morning to you!

Today I am going to tell you a true story about how prayer works in our lives. The story took place many years ago when I was a child.

I awoke one morning very excited. My uncle was driving my mother and me all the way to Indiana to visit my grandmother and the rest of the relatives. This trip had been in the planning stages for weeks, and today was the day. This may not sound out of the ordinary today; however, it was the late 1930's. Automobiles were not as commonplace as today, especially in New York City, and it was a treat to ride in one. My excitement was short lived when I realized I did not feel good. When my mother came in to wake me, I dreaded telling her, but she had a sixth sense and knew by looking at me that something was wrong. Mother had one solution for all discomfort- enemas! She was sure once that was taken care of we would be on the road. As the day went on however, I was not any better and experienced a definite pain in my side. She called the doctor and he said he would be at the house just as soon as office hours were over. Unfortunately, this would not be until late afternoon. By this time, I was doubled over in pain. When he arrived, he took one look at me and instructed my mother to get me to the hospital immediately. I did not take this news joyfully. You see, I just knew that if I went to the hospital I would die. Everyone died in the hospital. As my father carried me down the steps of the apartment building, I screamed, "I don't want to die!" It was much later in life, after I had my own children that I realized what a horrific memory this must have been for them.

As soon as the surgeon opened me up, he saw that my appendix had burst, and the infection had spread. In order to make sure it was all out, the doctor inserted a drain in my stomach. The operation appeared to be a success, and according to my mother, when she came to see me the next morning, I was sitting up in bed talking a blue streak. However, her sixth sense was working overtime and she did not like the way I looked. She told the nurses who in turn said that was expected after surgery.

That evening when my parents returned to the hospital, they found me in an oxygen tent. My temperature had spiked. For the next two weeks, it was touch and go. I have no memory of that time except for the hallucinations that I still recall to this day. I was lying in my hospital bed and the whole floor was having a big party. I was not invited. People were laughing, and joking, and drinking orange Mission soda (this in itself is a mystery; I do not recall ever drinking Mission soda, and orange was not a favorite flavor of mine). I kept begging for something to drink, but all they would do was show me the bottle and go on with their partying. Another hallucination I had was of a chubby friend named Phyllis; she was sitting on my chest and would not get up, no matter how much I yelled. Both of these were understandable since I was extremely thirsty from the fever and my labored breathing.

My temperature escalated to 108 degrees (this was reported in the medical journals). Packed in ice, I had tubes running in and out of my body, and needed several blood transfusions. My mother, exhausted from worry and lack of sleep, proved to be the donor. My grandmother, aunt, and uncles flew up from Indiana steeling themselves for a funeral. Finally, the day came when the doctors took my parents aside and said they had done all they could, and it was just a matter of time. By this time, my mother was beside herself with grief. She told me later that she left the floor, went up to the roof and stood staring up at the sky. She raised her fist and exclaimed, "I can't take this anymore! If you are going to take her, then do it now or leave her here!" Spent from hysterical sobbing, she returned to the floor and met by the doctor. He rushed over to her and exclaimed, "I have been looking all over for you. Your daughter's fever just broke. She is going to be all right."

When Mother told me what had transpired during my two-week delirium, I immediately thought God had saved me for greatness. Looking back on my life, I cannot say I have achieved this end, but I can say I have had wonderful experiences teaching how God does work in our lives. As a teacher, I cannot leave this story without doing what comes naturally.

In the Aramaic, the language that Jesus spoke, the word that was translated as "ask" really means "claim" when Jesus instructed us to "ask believing," He meant we were to *claim our good*. It is our right as God's children to act and know that all the Father has is ours, all His love, wholeness and life. He grants all prayers asked with "passion"; it is the intense passion, which imports belief. When we are not sure of a thing, we appear ambivalent. When we are on the fence, we show indecision. When we know, we put our heart and soul in the knowing; when we know, we have faith.

I am sure that mother prayed during the two weeks that I was so ill. I am equally sure she was not hesitant as to what outcome she wanted. However, I know she was unclear as to *how* God would answer. As soon as she gave up, so to speak, she demanded an answer. He heard. Her plea was a claim for my life; the demand for it proved she believed in His Power. Unknowingly, her prayer was a prayer of conviction.

Faith works miracles even when we do not know we are using it. I realized this early on because of my experience. When you have faith in the power of God, miracles happen!

Before I leave this morning, let me answer the unspoken question. Yes, God *does* answer all prayers of the heart. By that, I mean what you truly desire is what you receive. Sometimes we fool ourselves into thinking we want something, but in our hearts, we know it may not be so. We fail to listen to 'the voice within,' to our intuition, or just plain common sense. Then when our prayers 'appear' to go unnoticed, we cry, "God is at fault." I am here to tell you "*know* what you want-truly want-*believe*, have faith enough to *claim* it as rightfully yours, and so it will be."

God bless you!

CHAPTER II:
Heart's Desire

Good Morning:

    I am sure you have heard that there are no such things as accidents. At one time, I may have disagreed with you. You see, I thought I came into the ministry by accident. A neighbor invited me to attend an astrology class. That subject had always fascinated me; however, the teacher turned out to be even more intriguing. Here was a woman of very meager means who lived in a little house whose only income was from a small social security check and the classes she taught. However, she had an aura about her of peace and love, and, as I watched her, I envied her quiet acceptance. At this time in my life, I was restless. I was searching for something, or maybe something was seeking me. I was open and ready to explore different avenues. One evening, after class, she announced that she also conducted meditation classes and invited us to attend. I thought that if meditation was giving this woman the peace she exuded, then maybe it would help me too. I attended the meditation class, which proved to be enlightening. She taught the class how to meditate, giving us the steps to quiet the mind, but instead of the peacefulness I searched for, my restlessness seemed to intensify. I questioned her about it and her answer was to seek my heart's desire. I told her that was no consolation, that if I knew my heart's desire I would not be so muddled.

    She then asked me, "What is it you like to do better than anything else?"

    I answered, "Sing."

    Her reply, "What do you like to sing?"

    Much to my astonishment, my immediate response was "hymns" but I had not attended church in years. After some discussion, we concluded that maybe I needed to be in a gospel group. I certainly enjoyed listening to them and the music stirred my soul, so I began looking for a group to join or fellow singers to begin one. Every time I thought I was close, it did not work out. I was getting quite frustrated. Then one Sunday, she took me to a Unity Church service and my whole life changed.

Let me inject here an example of how invested we humans are in our beliefs. I was raised a Baptist, sang in the junior and senior choir, was involved in church activities and baby-sat for the minister and his wife. As I sat in the Unity Church on that first visit, I looked around for the minister. Not seeing *him*, I asked my companion where he was; it was at that moment a woman walked down the aisle toward the pulpit and I received my unbelievable answer: This church had a female minister! As I watched her and listened to her, I was in a state of shock. The idea never occurred to me because "everyone knew *only* men could be ministers;" at least that was the implication. I sat there enthralled. She was a wonderful speaker. She was reaching the people. She was bringing the Bible to life. That was the beginning of 'the renewing of my mind.'

It was not that Sunday, and maybe not the next, but very soon after, I was sitting in the congregation, and distinctly heard a voice saying, "That is what you are to do." My quest was over. I had found my heart's desire.

Unity's basic textbook written by Emily Cady is entitled *Lessons in Truth*. In it, she explains that desire is God tapping at the door of your heart. When we discover the strong desire within and what it is we are to do, the way is made straight; not always unproblematic, but guidance is assured. Ahead of me, the road would not be easy, nor would it happen overnight. Once I knew what I was to do, my hand was to the plow and there was no going back. I did not know how to achieve it and, frankly, did not wholly believe it, but Spirit was moving me along the path.

The path was very rocky and, at times, discouraging. Soon after, I received the 'insight' to my desire; my husband accepted a new job and we relocated to Lake Park, Georgia. It was a beautiful town but the location was far from what would bring me my heart's desire. We lived in between two Unity churches, both 100 miles away in opposite directions. I began commuting to the one in Tallahassee, Florida. The minister was founding a new Unity church there, and I thought it would be a good opportunity for me to learn. I continued taking classes and traveling to Unity Village in Missouri for extensive courses. A year or so later, the minister asked if I would like to speak on Sundays while he took an extended honeymoon. From the very first Sunday I spoke, I was in my element, and I knew that all would be well.

When the minister returned, he asked me if I would be willing to take over a small group in Panama City, Florida. I had completed all courses, and was now a Licensed Unity Teacher and this qualified me to lead the group. I was excited about the prospect but informed him and the group that I would be applying to ministerial school, and my time there would be temporary. Several months later, it was time for my interview, and I was flying high.

At that time, the Licensing and Ordination Committee interviewed each applicant on a one to one basis for approximately twenty minutes. I knew instinctively, before the end of the first interview that I did not stand a chance, but I persevered. I continued to have hope and faith as I waited patiently at the mailbox for what I desperately desired-my letter of acceptance. The letter came, but it was a denial. Believe me when I say I sank to the depths of despair. I cried. I ranted. I raved, "Why? Why? I had the desire!" This is what I thought was asked of me. What was I to do now? All my hope appeared dashed. My faith shaken I fell into a deep state of depression. Without a goal, without something to strive toward, I felt my life was over. I had been so happy with the prospect of teaching and serving others-to be able to bring to others what I had found and believed to be the Truth about our relationship to our Creator, and the meaning of life.

If we would only listen, God continually speaks to us. He uses people, books, and even songs we may hear on the radio to give us the message we need to hear. I received such a messenger when I forced myself to go to church in Tallahassee that following Sunday morning. I knew my fellow parishioners would ask me about the outcome of the interviews, and I dreaded it. I also knew I had to face my friends and fellow students eventually. They were very supportive and, after receiving consolation and being encouraged to keep trying, I headed home with the tears flowing. In the rear view mirror, I suddenly saw the flashing lights of a police car. Raised in a society that feared and respected authority, I was very concerned about being pulled over, especially since I did not know why.

The police officer came to the car and said, "Do you know you were going thirty-five in a twenty-five mile zone?"

I said I did not and apologized. *My dear messenger from God* then said to me, "I will not give you a ticket, but I will tell you <u>to slow down</u>. I must admit it did take me a few days to realize he was giving me an encouraging message, but once the clouds lifted from my mind, I saw clearly. However, I was still not sure of the next step, and one morning, trying desperately to get some direction, I began my morning meditation with tears flowing and frustration mounting, I screamed into the silent living room, "What do you want me to do?" The phone rang almost immediately, and it was a member of the Panama City group requesting that I come back to teach. I had said my good-byes to them, thinking I would be accepted at school. This was my answer. I immediately said yes.

It was five years of ups and downs. I moved to Panama City rented a house in which we held Sunday morning services and we began to grow. We had started out with twelve eager people and within a year and a half were fifty strong. Those dedicated in my congregation stepped out on faith and we purchased our church home. Four years later, I was licensed as a Unity minister and the following year, in 1984, ordained by Exception as founder of the Christ Unity Church in Panama City, Florida.

When I had gone for the original interview with the Licensing and Ordination committee, the last minister on the committee said to me, "Joanne, remember if Spirit wants you here, nothing can keep you away." Was this another message from God? I honored those words and kept them in my heart. I did not get my heart's desire *the way I thought I would*, but God was working in my life; He *was* directing my path.

Once you know your heart's desire, picture it. See yourself doing it when you wake in the morning and as you fall off to sleep at night. When you pray and meditate, know God is working within you to give you your heart's desire. Do not get discouraged. Change, order, desires, may take time to manifest in your life. God does not test us; we test ourselves, and it is quite possible that when we do not see results 'yesterday' we begin to doubt. It is those very doubts that will hold back our good.

I came across this story, written by Emmet Fox. In closing this morning, I would like to share it with you.

Don't Hurry the Chicken

A little city child was spending his vacation on a farm. They showed him a hen sitting on a nest of eggs, and told him that some day a little chicken would come out of each egg. The child was delighted at this dramatic idea, and every morning he went around expecting to see the miracle occur.

Days passed, and nothing happened. The eggs still looked exactly the same. Not the slightest change occurred in the appearance of things, and gradually his faith waned. At last one day he gave up hope altogether, and told himself bitterly that he had been deceived, and nothing would ever happen.

Next day, however, from habit he went around to the nest as usual, but without any hope; lo, and behold, it was his joy to see a group of beautiful little chickens running about.

Of course, wonderful changes had been taking place all the time, behind the shells, but there was nothing to show for it until the very last moment when the little chicks suddenly emerged complete and perfect.

Some of our greatest demonstrations come to us like this. For a long time there is no change to be seen in the outer, but if we keep our faith strong, in spite of appearances, the demonstration will come-if at the thirteenth hour.

In this story, it was the spectator who lost faith, and so it did not matter. If the mother hen had lost her faith-well, there would not have been any chickens. Give your demonstration time to hatch. Keep your faith in God.

Taken from *Make Your Life Worthwhile*-p163

So you see, dear ones, you can have your heart's desire, but you must persevere and not lose faith. Expect it *Now!* Know that in God's time it will come. When all conditions are right for you, it will be.

God loves you and so do I.

CHAPTER III:
PROOF OF GOD AT WORK

The beginning pages of this chapter contain clarification on how we obtained our first church home. I felt it important for you to know what perseverance, determination, and love can accomplish, and how it all came together to further "my heart's desire."

Our little church group of twelve was growing. We met in the living room of my home, and every Sunday the room appeared to get smaller. There was no question that we needed to move, but where? On a whim, I called a real estate agent and asked him what was available to meet our needs. He asked me if I wanted a church building. "Silly man," I thought. I would love a church building but my expectation had not risen to such a height. I was thinking more of moving to a larger house. We made an appointment to look around at what might be available.

A few days later, after looking at a few definite no's, he drove to a building that, from the outside looked suspiciously like a church. It was an answer to a dream. It was a small building with a steeple on the roof and a huge double doorway. As we went inside, he told me it was originally a Mormon church. It had been sold to a furniture-refinishing factory. As a result, the whole inside had been gutted. There was varnish streaked everywhere from floor to ceiling; heavy-duty wiring hung from various points of the ceiling; the kitchen had been turned into a room to store and mix different paints. I wouldn't dare try to describe the bathrooms, of which thankfully, there were two. You know the saying, "Beauty is in the eye of the beholder." I fell in love. Here was our church. The possibilities were fabulous, but would anyone else see what I envisioned? The first test was the board of directors. I was blessed with a board with the same vision as mine, and they agreed.

The second test would not be as easy. The congregation was a group of loving people, seeking to learn and know, but there were those who still judged by appearance, and we needed both emotional and financial support from them. I can still see the look on their faces when they came to see what we hoped would be our new church home. Some were fine with it; however, there were those who had reservations but would accept the majority decision. Then, there were those who <u>only</u> saw a colossal mess and a lot of work. Not only did they want no part of it, they felt it was an impossible feat. After quite a few weeks of discussion and planning, we were able to get the support needed to raise the down payment. We had the go-ahead.

It is an amazing thing how people will rally together for a cause. About twenty angels pitched in on Saturdays and during the week as time allowed. The floors, walls, and ceilings needed scraping and painting. The kitchen needed a complete remodeling with countertops, sink, stove and refrigerator. The rewiring had to be completed, and carpeting installed. The appliances and carpet were either donated, bought at garage sales, or purchased from merchants who lovingly gave us a discount. Those special members whose vision for our church was greater than its actual appearance did all the work.

Then came that special day in March of 1980 when the doors of "Christ Unity Church of Panama City" opened for the first time. I said earlier, I still remember the look on the faces of the dissenters but it will never compare with their faces on that morning! As the people walked in and looked around, they realized what had been accomplished-their faces held expressions of awe. They could not believe the transformation. It was further proof that when one is on the right track, God opens all stops to provide.

I wrote a special message for that Sunday - a message on Faith because that was the cornerstone of our church. The message is still special to me and whenever asked to speak at a church, this is the message I deliver. It brings back the same glorious moments that I felt on that day. It was too long ago to remember how or why I came up with this idea. It is a paraphrase of a well known children's tale and I sincerely hope you will not only enjoy it, but receive the message it contains in the same vein it is given.

The Three Pigs

Once upon a time, there were three pigs. One day, they decided to strike out on their own, and live separate lives. The first little pig decided to build his house out of straw, and when it was completed sat in his house complacent in the knowledge that he was safe and secure. One night there was a knock at the door, and he heard a booming voice saying, "Let me in or I will huff and, puff, and blow your house in." The little pig was terrified, and as the wind became stronger, and his house began tumbling down around him, he ran out the back door, straight to his brother.

Now his brother had built a house out of sticks, and he too was confident and felt safe and secure. Had he not built his house with his own little feet? He had picked and placed every stick; what could possibly destroy it? He heard his brother squealing at the front door crying, 'let me in' and saying, "There was a gruff voice, and a big wind came along and blew down my house. I was scared so I came here to be safe." The brother opened the door, and tried to calm him. He told him he was safe - that nothing could blow down *his* house. For a while, at least, it looked as if he were right. Then one night there came the knock at the door and the big booming voice declaring, "Let me in or I will huff, and puff, and blow your house in." They looked out the window and saw this big wolf huffing and puffing, and suddenly the house began to shake. The two little pigs jumped and ran as fast as their little feet would carry them for the "devil himself" was after them. At least, that was what they believed so they headed straight to their big brother's house.

Now here was a pig that had seen a bit of the world. He read, listened, continually sought knowledge and, most of all tried to apply it to his everyday life. When it came time to build his house, he did his research and concluded that brick would be his best bet. His home was solid; it was on a strong foundation. Inside it was warm, cozy, and full of light. He was happy. At the sound of the knocking at his door and the excited voices, he opened it to see his trembling brothers on his doorstep. He bid them enter and tried to soothe their fears. He told them there was absolutely nothing to be afraid of but they were too frightened to listen. Again, the big booming voice-the wolf was at the door. The two brothers ran and hid under the bed for there was no place else for them to go. This was it; this was the end. The older pig put out the light, and with a knowing smile on his face, went into the bedroom, crawled into bed, and fell fast asleep safe in the knowledge that no-thing could hurt him or his house. No plague would come to his dwelling.

The first little pigs name was Disbelief. He grew up not believing in anything except what his senses told him. If he could see it, touch it, or hear the results of something from another, then it was gospel. If the sky looked black, it would definitely rain. There was no possible way for the sun to shine and the sky to clear. He went to church on Sunday, and although there was something within nudging him to listen, he would hear the message, but forget it as soon as he passed through the church doors. He lived in a world of negation - a world of dog eat dog, a world in which he felt he must strike while the iron was hot. As the years progressed and old age took over, and he no longer had a job, maybe his reasoning or motor capabilities would lessen and all would be lost. His life would be over. And so it was, at the first sign of trouble, he ran to his brother. Surely, his brother would protect him.

His brother's name was Belief. He was always trying. He would sit and ponder, "What goes on in the invisible? What or who made the world? How does it stay in place? Who is pig? What is pig?" His mind was full of questions. He would read and believe. He would go to church on Sunday, and after the message that he listened to most carefully, would join in conversation with his fellow pigs. He would speak positively, and give lovingly to those around him. However, without realizing it, every now and again, negative statements would pass from his lips. He did try.

When he heard his brother crying and saw him shaking at the front door, when he spied the wolf huffing and puffing, and felt his house begin to shake, all the accumulated 'intellectual' knowledge that he had acquired was forgotten. Afraid, he grabbed his brother and ran to the only protection he could think of – his other brother.

The third little pigs name - have you guessed it? - was Faith! Faith grew up embracing the world. Faith <u>knew</u> there was a power greater than he was, and he could find and use this power. He was aware it would take hard work and discipline, but the desire was great within him. He would not allow <u>any</u> outside force to sway or distract him. Faith was single minded. He held to the truth he heard in church, "God is the One and Only Power in the Universe." He held that idea until it became a knowing throughout his whole being; it became part of him. It was not so surprising when fear in the shape of a wolf came to blow his world apart, he knew with every fiber of his being that it would pass. He was protected.

It is written: *"Then said Jesus unto his disciples, 'if any man will come after me, let him deny himself, and take up his cross, and follow me. For whosoever will save his life shall lose it; and whosoever shall lose his life for my sake shall find it."* (Matthew 16:24, 25) Jesus, the man, Christ the Spirit, gave instructions to all who would follow Him, not in a demanding or commanding way, but by simply saying this is the way; it is up to you.

Disbelief says," What is this Christ? Surely, if it exists, it is not for me. I am a mere pig. I do not have time to search for something as intangible as "things of the Spirit."

Belief says, "Christ? I know who and what it is. It is the Spirit of God indwelling in me, guiding, leading, and teaching me. I know when I remember, He is there, but I do forget!"

Faith says, "Thy will be done. I of myself can do nothing. I deny that part of me which is ruled by my senses. I deny that part of me that is personality, which demands attention, demands its way. I shall not lose my life to the eccentricities of the ego, instead I give way to the Spirit within, the Christ, and I am reborn."

The human consciousness takes itself far too seriously and is unhappy a great deal of the time. When our pride gets hurt, our feelings ruffled, or our dignity attacked, we then get insulted. Why? Because we live in sense consciousness, are centered on an earthly plane, and do not realize our spiritual heritage.

In the Old Testament, Jacob wrestled with his adversary and that adversary was both friend, and foe. Isn't this true of every challenge? Before we find the solution, it appears to defeat us, bring us down. We worry, fret, and feel, "this can't be." Then comes the moment we face it, work through it, and with a deep breath, realize the peace of accomplishment. The adversary is an opportunity for growth. It opens the way for a time to discover who and what we truly are - an Expression of God, a Spiritual Being. We hurt ourselves when we identify with the sense of me and mine.

Lao-tzu said, "He who feels punctured, must have been a bubble." When we realize how divine thought is, how magical it is, that it is 'our thoughts' which govern us, we can stand tall, straight, and strong. We are able to fear no-thing, and no one. Persistence in this realization brings with it the recognition that someone else's thought has <u>absolutely no power</u> over us, <u>unless</u> it becomes (or already is) our <u>own thought</u>. Our well-being depends on our own ideas, concepts, and beliefs, on our own consciousness. Everyone is under the governance of his/her own thought and no other. This principle, this Law, is God's gift to all. The government is the Kingdom of God; the Kingdom of God is within you! *"Neither shall they say, Lo here! or, lo there! for, behold, the kingdom of God is within you."* (Luke 17:21)

When I started attending Unity-after class one evening, I remember debating with a fellow student on the power of faith. I believed and still maintain that faith will move mountains, that faith will keep us safe, and secure, no matter what the appearance. I debated the issue that if one was to take poison, it would not kill him <u>if he knew in his heart it would not</u>. He would know, *"According to your faith be it done unto you."* (Matthew 9:29) Of course, it goes without saying, that a Truth student would not deliberately do this.

The psalmist said, *"A thousand shall fall at thy side, and ten thousand at thy right hand; but it shall not come nigh thee."* (Psalms 91:7) Each of us have had strife, some more than others. The purpose is to awaken our understanding. As it grows, suffering diminishes. It is possible to stand apart from the law of averages; it is possible to live your life encircled by prayer, knowing it shall not come nigh you! It is possible to have the winds of fear blow to hurricane velocity and stand before it unafraid because of the firm foundation of faith.

I began this talk with the story of the three pigs. Forgive me for taking license in naming them, Disbelief, Belief, and Faith, and the wolf, Fear. I did this to make a point, which in turn brings up a question. What causes one to be, as our first pig, unbelieving in all things and what causes the other extreme, the pig that knows no fear only unshakable faith? I have a theory I would like to share with you. From our earliest recollection, most of us learned there was a God. Some taught He was punishing as well as bountiful. We were told He was our Father. The Lord's Prayer begins with the two words, *Our Father"* and there is the rub. Some of us have had, or do have father's who did show love, and were kind, fathers who took the time to say, "Hey, a mistake is a mistake, try again." who said, "You're a great kid, keep up the good work." Those who were lucky enough to have had this experience can easily transfer to a loving Supreme Being that uplifts, leads, and guides. However, how about those who had no father, or maybe had one who was unwittingly cruel, who did not show faith in the child's ability or appeared to be disinterested? Maybe the man had so much on his mind trying to make a decent living for his family that he could not give the time and attention the child needed. Whatever the reason, how can this child relate to the loving invisible father when he cannot relate to the one he can see? How can this child reach out and know-in the invisible realm, there is a Being that is all providing, all knowing, and always ever-present? How can that child grow into adulthood believing in a loving source of good that will abundantly take care of him? It seems to me, he/she would find it very difficult; so, those of us who have been fortunate to know and discover the Truth of the Omnipresence, Omniscience, Omnipotence of our Father-Mother God must be an example of this Truth.

By being a good neighbor, and friend, we must help others to know that God our Father is always there, help them to know that God the Father encircles everyone in His love, help them by accepting, loving, and forgiving others, as we are accepted, loved and forgiven. We can assure them that God protects us from all harm and teach by example to look not to appearances, but to have faith in the promise, *"it shall not come nigh thee."* (Psalm 91:7)

Jesus, the Christ, walked the earth as a teacher, our teacher, our way-shower. He promised we could do what he did, and more. He said He was not the great one; it was the Father within Him that doeth the work, and the Father was/is within us all.

Which little pig would you wish to live with? Would you choose Disbelief, in a house of straw, a house that will topple at the first appearance of fear? Belief, in a house of sticks, one that will stand only as long as one does not listen to fear, or will it be with Faith in a house so strongly built that no-thing or no one can destroy it?

"Because thou hast made the Lord, which is my refuge, even the most high, thy habitation; There shall no evil befall thee, neither shall any plague come nigh thy dwelling. (Psalms 91:9.10)

May God Bless you in this realization; God loves you and so do I!

CHAPTER IV:
What Is New Thought?

Before going on, this might be the right place to delve into the background of the New Thought Movement. Phineas Parkhurst Quimby was the Father of New Thought in America. It is a spiritual, religious, philosophical movement that had its beginning in the nineteenth century. Quimby was born in Lebanon, New Hampshire in 1802. He spent most of his life in Belfast, Maine, and died there January 16, 1866. In 1830, he began questioning and developed his system for Spiritual healing. He believed he had discovered the secret of healing performed by Jesus the Christ and went on to prove it. He realized the Truth of his being- Oneness with God- and taught it to others.

Mary Baker Eddy, a patient who became his student, was the founder of Christian Science. Through the indirect teaching of Phineas Parkhurst Quimby, the direct teaching of Emma Curtis Hopkins, an associate of hers, and her own explorations, Mary Baker Eddy became the "teacher of teachers." Among her students were Charles and Myrtle Fillmore, co-founders of the Unity Movement. They later became students of Emma Curtis Hopkins and were ordained by her.

Unity had its beginning in 1889 with the publication of "Modern Thought," a magazine that is published today under the name of "Unity Magazine." Ernest Holmes founded the movement Religious Science in 1927. In collaboration with Nona Brooks, Malinda Kramer founded Divine Science in the late 1880's. The movement, Divine Science, was organized in 1898.

If it were not for Phineas Parkhurst Quimby and his insights, which continued to be nurtured by others, the New Thought Movement would not have occurred. His philosophy in one sentence was that "Man is just what he believes he is to himself."

The Unity Movement

The story of Charles and Myrtle Fillmore, co-founders of Unity, is one of difficulties, sickness and health, doubt and faith. It also points out what can be accomplished when we completely surrender to our spiritual nature. Following are two messages, one delivered on Mother's Day, the other on Father's Day, that give insight to their dedication.

Mother of Unity

Good Morning and a Happy Mother's Day to you!

Today I am going to tell you the story of our co-founder, Myrtle Fillmore. I researched this information from a book written by Thomas E. Witherspoon.

Mama Myrtle, as she was lovingly called by her co-workers, was born Mary Caroline Page on August 6, 1845, in Pagetown, Ohio. Her family was deeply religious. They attended a Methodist church, but at an early age, Myrtle found some of the doctrine hard to accept. Her love for her parents prevented her from sharing her feelings; so she affirmed what she could accept, and denied what she could not. This is something I can identify with for as a child I could never accept the premise of a devil. Myrtle loved God and nature and would spend many hours in the woods alone. She was a sickly child, afflicted with tuberculosis, and heard all her life that she was delicate, needed to be protected, and must not overdo it. She loved education and was an avid reader. After high school, she attended college for a year. In those days, women could only go for one year. Upon graduation at the age of twenty-three, she received a license to teach and secured a job in 1868 in Clinton, Missouri. Myrtle stayed in Clinton only two years and, because of her health, moved to a dryer climate. She settled in Denniston, Texas where she met and married Charles Fillmore in 1881.

They moved many times, and three years and two children later, finally made their permanent home in Kansas City, Missouri. Meanwhile, her health was again declining, not only from the tuberculosis, but also from a malarial fever.

Myrtle had great faith in doctors and did whatever they told her to do. Her son said, "She was constantly dosing herself with medicines and made the whole family take the foul tasting stuff too."

Eventually, the doctors informed Charles and Myrtle that she had a short time to live. They considered moving again, but Charles had a dream that they should stay in Kansas City. The dream indicated that they would do great things and that their destiny depended on staying in Kansas City.

By the spring of 1886, Myrtle was very weak, and it appeared death was imminent. The Fillmore's heard of a lecture to be given by a Dr. Weeks, a student of Emma Curtis Hopkins, founder of the Illinois Metaphysical College, and decided to attend. As she sat there listening, she heard the one sentence that dramatically changed her life. "<u>I am a child of God and I do not inherit illness.</u>" She did more than hear it; she took that one sentence, and with all her conscious strength made it a part of her. All her life, she had heard and believed that she was born to be ill, suffer, and <u>die prematurely.</u> She now began to deny it. She took in those words of Truth, "child of God," and began to talk to her body. She acknowledged it was God's gift and His gifts were all good. Days, weeks, months went by and she gradually began to improve. She closed herself in her room and studied the four gospels. She placed an empty chair next to hers and "saw" Jesus sitting there. She knew He was there supporting and encouraging her. She repeatedly read from John:

> *"Verily, verily, I say to you. He that believeth on me, the works that I do shall he do also; and greater works than these will he do; because I go unto my Father" (14:12)*

> *"Therefore I say unto you, What things soever ye desire, when ye pray, believe that ye receive them, and ye shall have them." (Mark 11:24)*

> *"Wilt thou be made whole?" (John 5:6)*

She accepted what she read; she believed what she read. Her faith made her whole. In 1888, she experienced complete healing.

I would like to point out as human beings we are impatient creatures. There may be some who would ask, "Why not an instantaneous healing?" When we ask for healing or prosperity, we want it yesterday, forgetting it took time to get to the place where we are in need, and that it takes equal time to get to that place where we accept healing. This acceptance creates the manifestation. Because it takes time, there are those who begin to doubt, even give up, instead of holding firm knowing, *"as you believe you shall receive."* Myrtle had the patience and diligence to accept her healing in God's time. And so it was!

Myrtle's transformation was not only physical, but also mental and spiritual. Her consciousness (thinking and feeling) became so ingrained in Truth, in God, that she fully expressed what she believed. She developed the ability to heal all kinds of dis-ease. Below are several of her reported healings.

A neighbor who lived across the street, Mr. Caskey, was crippled and walked with crutches. They prayed together often. He did not understand healing was possible. She would instruct him-"put down your crutches and walk." He would remain doubtful. Then one day he suddenly realized what she was saying. "Have faith and walk!" He believed in the power of those words; he cast down the crutches, and walked across the room.

The Fillmore's had a laundress who suffered with asthma. Myrtle taught her how to pray positively, they prayed together and she was healed.

There was a salesman who came to their house; he saw young Lowell, Myrtle's son, and remarked he too had a son his age, but his boy would never see. Myrtle's immediate reply-"Don't say that. Your boy is a child of God. As a child of God, it is his right to see." To which he replied, "But the doctors say he will never see again." She wanted to know if he had ever prayed for his son, emphasizing that God heals. The salesman, seeing how strong her faith was, asked if she would pray for his boy. She agreed, and said, the first time she saw the boy, the cataracts on the boy's eyes were "as the whites of an egg," but she was not discouraged. Myrtle did not waver. She prayed and told the boy to repeat over and over again that God loved him and His will for him was perfection which included perfect sight. In time, the cataracts disappeared and his sight was restored.

In 1897, Myrtle wrote her personal statement of faith:

I do not believe in evil; I believe in good.
I do not believe in sin; I believe in Truth.
I do not believe in want; I believe in abundance.

I do not believe in ignorance; I believe in intelligence.
There are no discords in my being; there is only peace.
My faith, understanding, and love, are becoming one.
"What God has put together, let no man put asunder."*

p185

She lived her faith; she proved her faith. Sickly as a child and repeatedly told she would die at an early age, Myrtle not only had a complete healing, but also lived to 86. Her transition, from earth to life eternal, was one of acceptance and completion.

In prayer, Myrtle asked Spirit how to be, in a more quiet way, active in life. Soon after that, she began to prepare for her transition. She told her close companions that she had done all she could on this plane, and would leave when God revealed the right time. A few weeks before her passing she told another friend, it would be soon, that it would be easier to work from the other side. On the Wednesday before her passing, she helped Charles lead the service as usual, went to work the next day, answered letters, and laughed and joked with co-workers. She spent that weekend picking apples and receiving callers.

She told her dear friend she was going to die in a day or so. Her friend said, "She was so calm, peaceful, and beautiful; she told me her work was done on this side and it was time to go." Two days later, Myrtle made her transition.

I believe it was her faith that started Unity. Her faith brought forth the miracles in and around her life, and in the lives of her loved ones. Her faith inspired Charles.

Know God is Blessing you now.

---

* A comprehensive biography can be found in <u>Myrtle Fillmore, Mother of Unity;</u> written by Thomas E. Witherspoon and published by Harper and Row.

CHAPTER V:
THE UNITY MOVEMENT (PART 2)

Good Morning, and a Happy Father's day to all dads here today!
On Mother's Day, we examined the life of Myrtle. Today being Father's Day, I feel it is only appropriate to delve into Charles' life.

SEARCH FOR THE FATHER

Henry Fillmore, Charles' father, was born in Buffalo, New York. It was here that his uncle, the first ordained Methodist minister in the state, established the first Methodist Episcopal Church. Millard Fillmore, his cousin, had been out of presidential office for a year when Henry finished his schooling and headed west, settling in St. Cloud, Minnesota. He became an Indian trader and married Charles' mother, Mary, in 1851.

Charles Fillmore was born August 22, 1854 and at the age of two was captured by the Sioux Indians. They only kept him a day, and he was too young to remember what happened that day, but he said he always had the feeling they used him for some sort of ceremony. Charles' early years were very exciting. He spent a lot of time at the Indian camps playing with the children, learning how to fish and hunt, pick berries and gather wild rice. The northwest was growing and he spent time not only with the Indians, but also with traders, trappers, and travelers of all types. At the age of ten, his father moved out and built a hut ten miles down the road. He was a retiring man and needed to be apart from the growing locale. His mother, aged twenty-five, became the sole support of Charles and his brother Norton. However, Mary Fillmore found it difficult to give her children a cultural education. She made sure they attended school, but the only religious training was the little she knew as an Episcopalian.

When Charles was ten he fell on the ice and injured his hip. There were no x-rays; therefore, the doctors did not know the extent of his injuries. The hip did not heal and Charles grew worse. Doctor after doctor treated him to no avail. His pain was constant and he developed complications. For two years, he fought the 'disease,' and when he could, he would hobble around on homemade crutches. However, most of the time he stayed in bed, weak and uncomfortable. One day the infection began to diminish. His strength came back and the pain eased; however, his right leg had stopped growing. Finally, he went back to school only to leave two years later to take a much-needed job as a printer's apprentice. Later on, he worked in a grocery store and a bank. It was in the bank that he made friends with Edgar Taylor. Edgar's mother was tutoring her son and agreed to tutor Charles also. She introduced him to Tennyson, Shakespeare, Shelly, and the Brownings. His favorites were James Russell Lowell and Ralph Waldo Emerson. This was evidenced later when he named one son Lowell, and the other Waldo. Mrs. Taylor's influence caused him to ask questions about theology.

At the age of nineteen, he left St. Cloud. He never gave a thought to his lameness. It did not occur to him that it would be an obstacle, and he held many jobs, one as a mule team driver. Eventually, Charles went into real estate, met and married Myrtle, and became very successful. They made their last move to Kansas City where he again thrived in real estate.

He was very significant in the development of the city. Today there are streets, Myrtle Avenue and Norton Avenue, which still have the names he gave them. The depression hit Kansas City, his business declined, and so did Myrtle's health. As reported in the Mother's Day message, there was despair, sickness, the last effort, and then the miracle of Myrtles healing. Charles' business was failing which gave him time to observe her. He watched her as she continued to sit in the silence (meditation), and witnessed her health improve. He saw her friends and relatives coming to her for prayer and leaving uplifted. A light coming from her fascinated him. He wanted to believe, but he was a businessman, and very skeptical. He decided there must be a practical side to spiritual healing and began studying. He studied not only metaphysics, but also religions from all over the world. He investigated

Buddhism, Hinduism, Theosophy, and the Rosicrucian philosophies. The difficulty of this undertaking is beyond our perception.

The year was 1880, and he said, "The muddle was so dense that for a time I was inclined to ridicule, yet I could not get away from the evidence of a great power back of a flood of contrary statements." He doubted, and was honest about those doubts when he said, "although I was a chronic invalid and seldom free from pain, the doctrine at first did not appeal to me." However, a time came when he decided, "in this babble I will go to headquarters, if I am Spirit and this God they talk so much about is Spirit, we can somehow communicate or this whole thing is a fraud." He followed his wife's example, and began praying continuously, attempting to get in touch with God. At first, there did not appear to be any results. Month after month, he would mentally affirm what he was told by others would open the way. It became a habit, which he began to enjoy. Slowly, he began to see results. His pain ceased, his hip healed, and grew stronger. The right side of his body was still very weak, and so he began to pray more intensely. Soon the hearing began to return to his right ear, and the vision to his right eye. It took years but finally the four-inch brace that he had worn on his right leg was removed. There had been no sensation on his flesh from his hip to his knee, but the feeling returned and the muscles filled out. It was a slow improvement but enough to inspire Charles to be diligent. This led him to do more and more Spiritual research.

In April of 1889, the first magazine was printed. Its continuous publication makes it the oldest in the United States. Charles taught, healed, counseled, and 'knew' his Father. He made Jesus Christ his friend, and when he found Christ, he found himself. His articles and books all teach one thing; there is One Source, One Power, God the Good Omnipresent.

I believe all denominations are seeking and striving for one goal - to know God. I also believe that not only New Thought students but all seekers are searching to experience God, and with His direction may achieve the conscious level Jesus Christ discovered. We need unity of the Spirit. The idea of oneness is important; the only other alternative is separation. These ideas will take root, grow in consciousness, and bear fruit. The idea of oneness will bring joy, health, peace, and freedom. The idea of separation is the cause of all ills and is bondage to lack, limitation and disease.

Joanne M. Dator

Now to a degree, we may need some limitation in this world but remember we are not of this world. We are Spiritual Beings like our Father who created us. God is Law and, as Law, unchanging, immovable. God does not feel or react. This is a comfort when one realizes that God always is and ever will be unchanging. As our personal living Father, God is individualized within everyone. Call upon Him and He will fill you with warmth and love.

The message this morning is simple. We can contact God. He lives in us as us. When we sit in the silence, we can feel His presence and hear His guidance. Charles did and if he did, we all can. It just takes perseverance and desire.

He was a skeptic and a businessman who demonstrated that everything he had researched was true. Prove to yourself that God is available; search for the Father and you will find Him.

Charles knew his findings to be a Spiritual Way of Life that would help everyone, and so named the movement "Unity," signifying, One with God, one with fellowman.

I love you, Happy Father's Day.

Taken from the book <u>Charles Fillmore</u>
by Hugh D'Andrade

CHAPTER VI:
THE UNITY MOVEMENT (PART 3)

BY THEIR FRUITS YE SHALL KNOW THEM!

Good Morning to you!

    The monument to Charles and Myrtle's faith, dedication, and beliefs, is Unity Village in Lee's Summit, Missouri. Originally, it was a farm that covered over 1400 acres of land; on it is a one hundred and sixty-five foot tower that can be seen for miles around. In the Silent Unity building, there is a lighted window, which glows twenty-four hours a day. It is a symbol that someone cares. Ministers in training, Spiritual leaders, and workers are there to receive phone calls and written prayer requests. When someone calls, the voice on the phone gives encouragement, inspiration, and prays with the petitioner. The request is passed on to another who sits in quiet prayer and meditation. The written prayer is then placed in a special file where the prayer work is continued for thirty days.

    There is an administration building which houses the largest Metaphysical Library in the world, and a cafeteria where neighboring people and tourists from all over the area frequent. The Daily Word and the Unity magazine, the oldest magazines in US existence, are produced in the printing plant on the property

    There are motels and cottages, and a new hotel recently opened. These are not only for the Unity students, but also for those who wish to participate in retreats, and vacationers who want to take in the beauty and peaceful atmosphere of the Village.

The doctrine is not new. In fact, the movement is based wholly on the teachings of Jesus The Christ. It revolves around the Truth that there is <u>One Power, One Presence in the Universe, God the Good Omnipotent.</u> Unity teaches that God's Presence is attainable, and if we will seek to find and know Him, God will reveal Himself.

It teaches that God is not a theory or a hope but that God is real. God is here now! We get into trouble when discouragement hits, and we doubt. A sudden tragedy or disappointment makes us think, "God has left!" However, God can never be absent from any of us. He is closer than hands or feet. His hands are our hands, His feet are our feet, He speaks through our voice. He was with us in the beginning and will be with us into eternity. He/She/It, whatever is more comfortable for you, is Infinite.

We have difficulty with the word infinite because we have <u>limited</u> minds. We think, see, and hear from a <u>limited</u> viewpoint. We see form, we use time as a reference, and according to our age, we either can or cannot. Sadly, we live in a material plane and place our trust in our senses, <u>but</u>, we are <u>not</u> of this world. We are <u>Spiritual Beings;</u> the Kingdom of Heaven and Earth has been given to us as <u>our domain</u>. Jesus, our brother, said He was about his Father's business, which was/is to teach us to love, to accept healing, to be a comfort to others, and to forgive. This manifest world is our learning place where we discover whom and what we are and, then, how we are to go about <u>our</u> Father's business. God is Omnipresent and lives within you as you, dear one. We contact Him through prayer. All it takes is perseverance and the desire to know Him as your Loving Source of all that is.

The Basic Principles of Unity are:

1. <u>God is all good and active in everything, everywhere.</u>
   There is One Presence and One Power in the Universe
2. <u>I am naturally good because God's Divinity is in me and in everyone.</u>
   God is individualized in each person as, The Christ consciousness, demonstrated by Jesus the Christ
3. <u>I create my experiences by what I chose to think, feel and believe.</u>
   Thoughts held in mind create after their kind. The Law of Mind Action

4   <u>Through affirmative prayer and meditation, I connect with God, and bring out the good in my life.</u>
    Prayer is the means to experience the Presence of God

It is through the practice of these principles that Charles and Myrtle succeeded in the founding of the spiritual movement known as Unity. They subsequently published many books and magazines, trained ministers who in turn founded churches, not only in the United States, but in Canada, England, Australia, Germany, Nigeria, South America, India and throughout the Caribbean.

Their devotion and perseverance has brought a new light to the world. For that, I am personally grateful.

CHAPTER VII:
BEFORE THEY CALL

Good Morning!

Several incidents in my childhood stand out. One I related in the message, "Ask and You Shall Receive." This happening occurred just two years later. I was eleven, and it was a carefree time - at least, it was in my era. All I wanted was be outdoors with my friends, playing the games of the day - jump rope, red rover-red-rover, hide-and-seek, and shooting marbles. The most fun was roller-skating, and in the early forties, there were not many automobiles, parked or cruising on our street so it was safe enough to skate up, down, and around the block. It was late in the afternoon on a fall day in early September, and my friends and I were having a grand time doing just that. It was a Friday, and every Friday my father would stay in the city, have dinner, and attend his weekly lodge meeting. As I skated by the house, my mother came out on the porch and called me in for supper. I must admit I was not the most obedient of kids and complacently kept rolling on. My mother had struck up a conversation with the next-door neighbor and was temporarily occupied, and I, seeing that my friends had already turned the corner, hurriedly skated after them.

To this day, I have a mind, which anticipates the consequences of my actions. As I was gaining momentum to catch up with my friends, I suddenly realized that I might not make the turn around the corner. At the speed I was going, I would have to cross the intersection and it was possible that a car could be coming just at that moment. I decided to do the only logical thing- jump up on the curb, stop myself, and grab the telephone pole. Quick as a flash, the next thought hit me. The telephone pole, made of wood, was full of splinters, and I dare not grab it. Jumping up on the curb, I lost my balance and went down on my backside full force. I looked around and thanked God that the kids did not see me fall. What a humiliation! Then I tried to get up, and the pain that shot though me was intense. There I sat not knowing what to do. I could see my mother on the porch, still in conversation. We lived half way up a very long block, and I knew I had to get home.

I took off my skates and, gritting my teeth, started walking home. Mother, watching me, thought I was walking with one skate on and one off - that is how much I was favoring my right leg. The pain was so severe I really do not know how I did it. I got to the steps of my home and could go no further.

There were five concrete steps to the landing and seven wooden steps lead up to the porch. There was absolutely no way I was going to make that. On top of that, I was a big girl, a bit on the hefty side, and my mother would not be able to help me into the house. I sat there with tears running down my face and silently cried, "Dear God, please bring my daddy home." It was at that moment; my mother looked down the street, and saw my father had turned the corner.

It is written in Isaiah 65:24, *"And it shall come to pass, that before they call, I will answer; and while they are yet speaking, I will hear."* That is exactly how I felt. My Heavenly Father knew I would have need of my earthly father. Something within told him not to go to the lodge meeting that evening, he would be needed at home.

God works in mysterious ways to give us our desires, to help in times of need; but unfortunately, we do not heed. I bet, dear ones, if you think back over your life you will discover there were times when circumstances were such that the seemingly impossible proved to be possible. Prayers are answered; all prayers are answered. There may be times we do not believe it because the answer did not come the way we wanted. However, it was our brother, the greatest teacher to walk the earth, Jesus the Christ, who said, *"Ask and it shall be given unto you;"* (Matthew 7:7)

Let me leave you with one last thought. I am sure you have heard of many miraculous feats. There have been stories of those who have lifted an automobile off a loved one or survived a fall from a great height. I had my miraculous feat that afternoon. The ambulance took me to the hospital, and after looking at the x-rays, the doctors discovered that I had slipped my hip out of the joint. Remember I had walked on that leg half a city block, which proves the strength, and fortitude one has when the need arises. Within is a great strength to be utilized whenever needed. All we have to do is ask, claim, and then receive.

God Bless.

CHAPTER VIII:
The Eleventh Hour

Good Morning!

    I have had many 'eleventh hour' experiences but have decided to relate the most recent one. A few years ago, I agreed to be minister of a small group in Northern Georgia. Before the final move, it was necessary to make several trips from Florida to cement arrangements and find a place to live. On my fourth trip, I was determined to find a house because time was of the essence, and I was eager to begin work. With the help of a newfound friend, the whole weekend was devoted to looking. I wanted and expected to find a house to rent. There will be more about this at the end of my story. However, the more we looked, the more discouraging it became. Finally, I succumbed and agreed to look at apartments. Again we hit brick walls-they were either to small, too expensive, or they did not allow pets. I tried not to look too discouraged. I told the group I would stay one more day but then I needed to get home. Monday morning, I looked in the paper and went to see about another place that was not to my liking. Resigned, I went back to where I was staying, packed my bag, and unhappily headed for the door.

    My hand was literally on the doorknob when the phone rang. The lady of the house was not home at the time and I debated whether or not to answer, but something told me I should. I picked up the phone; it was for me. The gentleman on the line said, "Have you found a place to live yet?" I informed him I had not and was just leaving to go home. He said he might have something for me; he was a real estate agent, and a friend of one the women in our group. We could go and see it right away.

    Before I go on, let me explain the significance of the events to follow. In Unity, we teach a class called Treasure Mapping. It is a simple exercise. All that one needs is a positive attitude, construction magazines. Once you have decided on what it is you desire, cut out of the magazine pictures that exemplify "exactly" your wishes. Written words further elaborate such as, "Thank you, Father." Be very careful about what you place on your map, as you will receive what you ask for; it is a Spiritual Law, "Thoughts held in mind create after their kind." What we hold in consciousness, what we believe, we will attract. In other words, if you are partial to a van but put a picture of an automobile on your map; you will get an automobile. Believe me. Let me emphasize here that intention plays a big part in this also. One must be of pure heart. By that, I mean we do not picture anything that is not for our good and/or the good of others. It is perfectly natural to desire more good in your life, and as I have said before, desire is God tapping at the door of your heart. Therefore, it is acceptable to put your desires down on paper where you can see them.

That is the point of Treasure Mapping. When it is completed, place it where you can see it several times a day, and as you look at it know, "It is Mine," and give thanks for it. It is also a good idea to place on your map some symbol of Spirit to remind you "all things come from God." There is another way if you do not wish to cut out pictures. Make a specific list, and head the list with, "Thank you for what I am about to receive," or words to that effect. The words must resonate from within your consciousness.

To go on, I had made a map several months before my being hired. Number one was a request for a ministry, next for my ideal home, which I explicitly detailed as follows: a three-bedroom home, full dining room, front porch, back porch, fireplace, garage, and a fenced in back yard for my dog. When the real estate agent pulled into the driveway of the rental house, I was ecstatic. Everything that I had listed was staring me in the face. Not only that but the neighborhood was quiet and beautiful- the one thing I had forgotten to include.

So, dear ones, another principle demonstrated. Earlier that day, I was going home to pack, and get ready to move with no place to go when I got there. However, at the eleventh hour, I received assurance that God was in charge and was taking care of me.   All was well.

Soon after my experience, my daughter had a similar one. She had a lovely three bedroom doublewide mobile home. It was across the street from the one I had owned. We are very close, and the daily reminder that I was several hundred miles away was depressing her. She wanted to move, but was told that it would be hard to sell her home, and that it would not be wise to look for a house until her mobile was sold. The real estate agent, who represented the trailer park, had sold my home, and she brought my closing check to my daughter. In the course of conversation, it came up that she wanted to sell also. The woman said she would keep her eye out for a buyer. A few days later, she called to tell my daughter that she had been on the Internet with a prospective buyer from Maryland who needed to relocate. He was very interested in her home, but he needed it immediately. My daughter said that this had come up so fast she could not possibly get out right away. They had not even looked for another place, let alone packed. However, what is meant to be will be. The gentleman asked if they could possibly move in two weeks. That very day my daughter called a friend in the real estate business and told her, she had to find a house "today." They started looking. It was proving to be a disappointing venture. Finally, my daughter asked to look at one house previously seen, but alas, it just did not hit the right cord. As they left the house and turned the corner they saw a for sale sign that had not been there before. They went in, and it was "the" house. It had been on the market only four days. The wife had already relocated and her husband was eager to follow her so my daughter and family could move in right away. It was a sale! The buyer of my daughter's house paid cash so there was no delay in loan application and he was satisfied with the price. At the 'eleventh hour' three families were provided for.

When we are aware, it is miraculous to see God working in our lives. I know there are those who would scoff and call it coincidence, but I am convinced there is a Higher Power in charge, and when we let go and allow it to work in our lives, "all things work together for good!"

God is Blessing you now.

CHAPTER IX:
Prayer and Meditation

The very first book I ever read in my Spiritual quest was, *Discover the Power Within You* by Eric Butterworth. He was an exceptional speaker, writer, and minister of the Unity Church in New York City. He begins his book with this story.

> According to an old Hindu legend, there was a time when all men were Gods, but they so abused their divinity that Brahma, the chief God, decided to take it away from men and hide it where they would never again find it. Where to hide it became the big question.
>
> When the lesser Gods were called into council to consider this question, they said, "We will bury it deep in the earth." but Brahma said, "No that will not do, for man will dig down deep into the earth and find it." Then they said, "Well, we will sink his divinity into the deepest ocean. But again Brahma replied, "No, not out there for man will learn to dive into the deepest waters, will search out the ocean bed, and will find it."
>
> Then the lesser Gods said, "We will take it on top of the highest mountain and there hide it." But again Brahma replied, "No, for man will eventually climb every big mountain on earth. He will be sure some day to find it and take it up for himself." Then the lesser Gods gave up and concluded, "We do not know where to hide it for it seems there is no place on earth, or in the sea, that man will not eventually reach."

Then Brahma said, "Here is what we will do with man's divinity. We will hide it deep down in man himself, for he will never think to look for it there." Ever since then, the legend concludes, man has been going up and down the earth, climbing, digging, diving, exploring, searching for something that is already within himself.

Taken in its entirety from the Prologue of *Discover The Power Within*, Eric Butterworth, author, published by Harper and Row, Publishers, Inc., New York, New York (1968).

This had a profound affect on me, although truthfully, I was not sure I understood it. I considered myself a religious person because of my love for God and belief in Jesus; however, my religious background was God "out there" and Jesus Christ, high on a pedestal. Prayer was very important, but I did not really believe God answered all <u>my</u> prayers. I definitely was not familiar with meditation and inner prayer. It was the early seventies and I had not yet begun my quest. Several years later, after completing my studies, November of 1979 to be exact, I was the spiritual leader of a group in Panama City, I wrote the following message on meditation. Since Unity was founded on prayer and meditation, I feel it is only right to begin this segment with that message.

"Silence is Golden"

Good Morning!

At least once a week, some one will mention to me that they would like to be closer in consciousness with God. Their need may be in the form of healing, prosperity, or just the joy of experiencing God. Expressing their desire, I feel I may not have expounded enough on the importance of meditation. Knowing the Truth of our being, what God is, and who we are, our relationship to each other, and to God, is recognized through experience - first the experience then the learning. As babies, we look at our hands, open and close them, grasp toys, and learn from the feeling. When we begin to walk, we fall down, and by experiencing the bumps and bruises, we learn to stay on our feet. As we progress on life's path, we go to school and take the necessary classes needed to prepare us for productive adulthood; this includes the highs of success as well as the lows of failure. Some of us go though this with a natural curiosity and others, like me, go through with clenched teeth. Once out of school, we can begin to "live."

That was my thought. I breathed a sigh of relief. I had my diploma; now I could get a job, earn my own living and be free. Freedom from what? For what? I had no idea. There was absolutely no thought of college in my consciousness-I had had enough of school. I settled into a routine, as did my peers, got a job, and dated boys, which led to an engagement and marriage. The next step was saving for a house and having children. Over the following years and throughout it all, a restlessness I could not define haunted me. Twice a year, I would redo the house, scrub walls, woodwork, change the furniture around, put up different curtains to brighten and give it a new look. But you know, after a few weeks, the restlessness would reappear. The questions would begin to haunt, "There has to be more to life than what I was experiencing." I started seeking. Because it is law, *"Seek and ye shall find,"* I did, although I must admit I did not realize immediately what it was that I found. Today, I thank God for my tenacity, my discipline, and my stubbornness.

I joined a meditation class, and, in the beginning, thought those around me were either crazy, putting on, or had great imaginations. I would sit in the silence with them and feel absolutely nothing while they would exclaim about the colors, and sounds, the peace and joy they felt. I continued in this manner for quite a while.

Did you ever stop to think how long it takes to learn something, let alone master it? When we had to learn our names and how to spell them, was it a matter of minutes, hours, days, weeks? When we had to learn arithmetic - adding, subtracting, multiplication, and division - if you were like me, it took several grades before it finally made sense. If you took up an instrument, long before you could play a tune, there were those intolerable scales. I studied singing, and you have to learn breath control, and practice 'oh's and ah's' up and down the scales repeatedly before you can begin an actual song, let alone perform. I studied Opera so you may well imagine how long it took to learn an aria. I am sure by now you have gotten my point. We can not know the Truth of our being, we cannot come to know who and what we are, we cannot know our relationship to God overnight. We need to become still, and regularly seek the Presence of God in the stillness.

Transcendental Meditation was very popular in those days, and I decided to try it. They give you a mantra - a word or words that do not make sense to you; this is to keep your mind focused. The teacher instructs you to sit in the silence and repeat your mantra twenty minutes in the morning and twenty minutes in the evening. For six months, I was faithful, and you know what- nothing, absolutely nothing, happened. Then one day, I had a breakthrough. It was a beautiful experience, and I can tell you in all honesty that if you remain faithful to the doing, you will come to know and realize Oneness.

Your degree of unfoldment, the depth of understanding, the acceptance of Truth, is entirely up to you. You determine the rate at which you receive. As you mastered the times table by repeating it over and over, so you will master the knowledge of 'Self,' by sitting in the silence and repeating your own mantra. This could be as easy as repeating God's name, Jesus' name, or a Truth statement, such as, "I am one with God." Meditation will open your consciousness and allow you to be on an intimate relationship with the Christ of your being. This frees you from the erroneous thinking of the carnal/mortal mind, and the belief in bondage to people, places, things, circumstances, and conditions.

We make contact with God through prayer, meditation, and transcendental meditation. Prayer is giving conscious attention to God. When we pray we are talking to God; we ask for blessings and give thanks for the receiving of same. Meditation is being still and listening to God. The word transcendental just means to move from one level of awareness to another. We are familiar with three of those levels. There is deep sleep, the dream state, and of course, the waking state. When we meditate, we rise to another level which 'transcends' the activity of the mind. This is the fourth level of consciousness, known as meditation or "sitting in the silence."

Just what is this silence? It is inner communion with God. I heard Sig Paulsen, a Unity minister, say at one of his lectures, "We should meditate more and medicate less."

I feel it is important for me to say, if someone has a health challenge, we do not in any way advocate <u>not</u> seeking medical advice. We know that God is the ultimate healer, and it is our faith that activates this power; however, we also realize one must have the conscious knowledge of this with every fiber of one's being. Therefore, Papa Charles (Fillmore) said, "Go first to God and then to man as God directs." If you feel the need for medical advice and treatment, then do as directed.

"*He that dwelleth in the secret place of the most High shall abide under the shadow of the Almighty.*" (Psalms 91:1) What is the secret place? Jesus referred to it as the "*...the kingdom of God within you.*"(Luke 17:21) It is a place where we rise above sense consciousness to be one with God in thought. Life is consciousness! We are the sum total of our beliefs, ideas, and conditions. Our consciousness is our sense of identity.

Jesus instructed, "*But seek ye first the kingdom.*" (Matthew: 6:33) There are many interpretations as to the whereabouts of the Kingdom. However, how can we misinterpret where the Kingdom is when Jesus told us, "*Behold, the Kingdom of God is within you.*" (Luke 17:21)? His instructions clearly are, "*...when thou prayest, enter into thy clos*et,.." (Matthew 6:6) meaning we are to close ourselves off, go into our own consciousness (mind), find the peace, the knowledge, the wisdom, the Kingdom, within. In doing so, we turn from the outer - from appearance- and give ourselves over to the Almighty.

When we meditate, it is important to surrender the part of oneself that worries, doubts, and fears. It is to be a time of peace and tranquil relaxation. There are those who use meditation purely for releasing stress; some use it to give them energy. However, for me, it is a time to seek and experience God. There is a barrier, an invisible wall, so to speak, which prevents us from remembering the Truth of our being, and it is in the stillness that we remove the barrier. We come away from the experience with a little more peace, a little more understanding, and with a little more Spiritual discernment.

There are no rules and regulations regarding meditation. It matters not how long one sits in the silence. It could be five minutes or twenty-five, the length of time spent is for our own awakening, not Gods. We are the ones that prayer and meditation will soothe, calm, and regenerate. The important thing is to make the contact. We enter with thoughts of God; we speak to Him, not in supplication, but as if, He is a friend sitting in the chair next to us. In the beginning, you will receive other thoughts crowding in and that is all right. Just let the thought finish, and then gently go back to your conversation or thoughts of God.

You can begin your journey into the silence by reading something inspirational, reciting the Lord's Prayer, or a favorite scripture. If none of these things apply, then try a mantra, using God's name or the name of Jesus Christ. This will quiet the mind and bring you peace.

Although I said there were no rules, relaxation is important. Tension and discomfort will always divide and disturb one's attention. Therefore, get into a comfortable position. Some people feel they must lie down; others say it is best while bathing; some will insist on being out doors; but you must find what is comfortable for you. I suggest sitting in a chair with one's feet on the floor and hands resting easily on one's lap. That is a recommendation only. As you get comfortable, if there is any part of your body which is tense, speak to it and tell it, 'be at peace.' Our bodies respond to a direct request for we have dominion over all. "*...and God said unto them ...replenish the earth, and subdue it: and have dominion ...over every living thing that moveth upon the earth.'*" (Genesis 1:28)

When we are relaxed, we feel healthy and whole. The Law is "Like Begets Like;" so, the more we can relax the more conducive to thinking positively which elevates us to a higher state of consciousness.

By seeking God, we become increasingly aware of all the good in our lives and around us. There will be changes in mind, body, soul, and affairs. However, I will not mislead you; these changes will not occur overnight. In practicing the Presence of God, it may take months before one experiences any differences, but, believe me, they are not only there, but you will know at the right time. It all depends on one's discipline, and belief system. Do not get discouraged and always be thankful for the opportunity to feel His Presence.

"*Blessed are the peacemakers: for they shall be called the children of God.*" (Matthew 5:9) Man is a Spiritual being, created in the <u>very image of God</u>. We can only realize and accept this Truth when we attune our minds with God. For too long, we have called ourselves "only human" and believed ourselves to be limited. We hear God is everywhere present, and at times, even claim Him to be within, but in times of stress we forget. Meditation gives us protection. It helps us to remember when we find we are in need. There is a Power within each of us that can and will come forth when activated. The above scripture states the peacemakers shall be call the children of God. Affirm, <u>You</u> are a child of God. Declare your Divinity. Believe it, and you will be a peacemaker- for He "*will go before thee, and make the crooked places straight:*" (Isaiah 45:2)

Through daily meditation, you will come to believe this more and more. I say to you this morning, have faith, pray without ceasing, keep the positive thought, learn to judge not by appearance, love, and above all, forgive; most importantly in everything, put God first.

I hear some of you saying, 'sounds good, but'…. my answer to you, I would never ask you to do what others have not already accomplished. I could not speak with authority unless I had already experienced what meditation can do.

To sum up, what is the silence? It is fulfilling the scriptures, *"Be still and know that I am…"* (Psalms 46:10) Get quiet and realize your Divinity. Give your mind permission to rest from the outer turmoil and to accept the peace within. Its purpose is to establish conscious communion with God. It is a way to find the Kingdom of God. Enter expectantly, knowing there is only One Presence and One Power in the Universe. *"But be ye doers of the word, not hearers only, deceiving your own selves."* (James 1:22)

If you truly desire God's blessings, you need to meet Him halfway. I leave you this morning with a quote from Thoreau:--

"If one advances confidently in the direction of his dreams, and endeavors to live the life which he has imagined, he will meet with a success unexpected in common hours."

Find God in the silence, within your own being, and I guarantee your life will change for the better.

God Bless You

PART TWO

CHAPTER X:
The Twelve Powers

Charles Fillmore strongly believed, and taught, there are twelve centers in the subconscious realm of man's mind. Each of these twelve centers is a power, which corresponds, or represents, one of the disciples; for example, Peter stands for Faith. It is my intention to introduce you to this mystical teaching by including in the book the following messages dealing with each of the Powers, and the disciple who represents them.

It is important to realize the significance of the number twelve as it appears throughout the Bible. There were the twelve sons of Jacob, the twelve tribes of Israel, and the twelve alter stones. (1 Kings 18: 31, 32) There is a reference to Jesus at age twelve; the Hebrew calendar has twelve months, and there are twelve signs of the Zodiac. Metaphysically, the number twelve stands for Spiritual fulfillment.

In Charles Fillmore's book-"The Twelve Powers", he wrote:

"The subconscious realm in man has twelve great centers of action, with twelve presiding egos or identities. When Jesus had attained a certain soul development, He called His twelve apostles to Him. This means that when man is developing out of mere personal consciousness, he begins to train deeper and larger powers; he sends his thoughts down into the inner centers of his organism, and through his word quickens them into life." (p.15)

It is not necessary for you, dear reader, to believe in the teaching of the Twelve Powers, but I would ask you to keep an open mind while reading the metaphysical teaching within the following messages.

Faith Your Inherent Power

Good Morning!

It is written; Jesus asked the disciples, *"Whom do men say that I the son of man am? And they said, Some say that thou art John the Baptist: some, Elias; and others, Jeremias, or one of the prophets.* (This, too, is one of the many examples of reincarnation left in the Bible. For if this were not a possibility, Jesus would have reprimanded the disciples for even thinking that He could be a prophet of old returned.) Jesus then asked, *"But whom say ye that I am?"* And Simon Peter answered and said, *"Thou art the Christ, the Son of the living God."* And Jesus answered and said unto him,

> *"Blessed art thou, Simon Barjona, for flesh and blood hath not revealed it unto thee, but my Father which is in heaven. And I say also unto thee, That thou art Peter, and upon this rock I will build my church: and the gates of hell shall not prevail against it. And I will give unto thee the keys of the kingdom of heaven: and whatsoever thou shalt bind on earth shall be bound in heaven: and whatsoever thou shalt loose on earth shall be loosed in heaven"* (Matthew 16:13-19)

It was not only the man, Peter, to whom Jesus gave this blessing, but also to what he represented - Faith! He gave that blessing to all who, using the Power of Faith, will receive what they asked for.

When Jesus reached a certain point in His development, He called His twelve disciples to him. Metaphysically, Jesus represents Spiritual Awareness, and the twelve disciples epitomize the powers that God has bestowed within man. Calling them to Him meant he was gathering the powers together to work <u>through</u> him. Each is located within a center of one's being. Faith, represented by Peter, is located in the pineal gland in the center of one's head. Faith is the ability to say "yes" to God with all your mind and heart.

There are those who live in the intellect and do not believe they can know God. There are those who think faith has something to do with a religious experience. Faith is a faculty, or a Power that we use in all phases of our lives. The fact that it is a Power is evident. People who have faith in their ability are more successful than those who do not. We call that confidence, but is not confidence a form of faith? It will accomplish wonderful things when given the right expression.

We are instructed, *"...If ye have faith as a grain of mustard seed, ye shall say unto this mountain, Remove hence to yonder place; and it shall remove; and nothing shall be impossible unto you."* (Matthew 17:20)

When we are faced with a challenge <u>if</u> we have solid faith in God, (through prayer) and believe (fast from doubt) in the Truth spoken by The Christ, we will be healed, challenges removed, problems overcome. Therefore, it is important to learn to cultivate faith through prayer, and use it knowing "God <u>will</u> do the work!"

We do use faith to some degree when we pray; otherwise, it is a useless ritual. Prayer and Faith go together. They develop in the same manner, in consciousness, through study, forgiveness, denying error, and affirming goodness. The development of faith is a bumpy ride for there are setbacks. Peter experienced his combinations of difficulties, steadfastness and wavering, victories and failures. Peter had been with Jesus for three years. They ate, slept, traveled together, and when asked at the trial if he knew Jesus, he denied-not once, but three times- any knowledge of Him. Is it any wonder that we have our tribulations? We are still in the process of learning and growing. Peter, awakened from the sleep of unawareness, exemplified that which he stood for-Faith. We, too, can release the splendor, let go the inhibitions, and move mountains (challenges that beset us) as we give total commitment to God.

It is important also to remember to hold fast to faith in whatever we are seeking, and in whatever we are doing <u>regardless of the appearance.</u> Everyone is seeking happiness, and desires to have a fulfilling, abundant life. When we are in harmony, we are happy and the opposite is equally true. This is due to the thoughts and ideas held in mind. It is a common belief that money, a loving family and friends will bring happiness, but things and people are not the root of happiness. Happiness comes from within. It is our mental thoughts and attitudes, which shape our well-being. Behind the fulfillment of every idea lies the amount of faith we put into it. Having faith in Universal Mind, having faith in our own capabilities, recognizing Faith as a power that is ours to develop and use, will guarantee the happiness we search for so longingly.

In order to accomplish this, it is necessary to center oneself in Universal Mind. It is here that success lies. We make the mistake of not realizing who and what we are, not giving credence to our Spiritual heritage. In Truth, we are "(in) the image and likeness of God." "*Let us make man in our image, after our likeness:*" (Genesis 1: 26) We miss the mark by not having faith in these words. The way to get back on course is to hold in mind and affirm the reality of God in all things and situations, and most of all, affirm our oneness with Him.

The divine idea of faith is introduced in Genesis 1:6 "*Let there be a firmament in the midst of the waters, and let it divide the waters from the waters.*" Water represents mind, the division being the conscious from the subconscious. To firm up means to build up the mind. Let us firm up the mind with the continual use of affirmations of Truth. Fill up the conscious mind with positive thoughts. In doing so, these thoughts seep into the subconscious mind where they set in motion and work to bring forth the good that is deserved. God's Presence keeps us safe, but it is our realization, our faith in Him and in His Presence, that provides the evidence.

It is through our thoughts and attitudes that we constantly make the conditions of our lives. I am sure you know people who are always complaining, "Life is against me." When things go wrong, their response is, "Oh it is always that way." I feel for those who fall back on Murphy's Law, "anything that can go wrong will," not realizing what they are claiming for themselves. This way of thinking builds a negative state of mind, and this is using faith wrongly. What we express is what we believe, and what we believe is what we demonstrate.

It is true that in life there can be some hard-hitting lessons we must learn. Life is a teaching process. When we were in school, the teacher handed out homework assignments; some were easy and some difficult. It was up to us to overcome the difficulty and pass, or not overcome and fail. Through events, encounters, and conditions, life does likewise, and it is important to keep in mind that attitude is the key. We have the choice to accept or attack whatever appears. Having faith in God is essential! Taking responsibility for the situation at hand, and not blaming every Tom, Dick, or Jane, will right any, and all wrongs. Begin by trying not to condemn or pronounce anything as evil, for what one thinks one attracts. Instead, have faith in the goodness of those around you. See God in the midst of every situation, and have faith in your Creator. All circumstances and conditions are temporary, and we waste so much time and energy fighting the appearance of so-called evil instead of embracing love, understanding, and faith.

When Jesus met Peter, his name was Simon, which means hearing. Metaphysically, this means he was ready and open to receive words of wisdom. The mind is a fertile, rich, substance in which ideas grow quickly. It is <u>our choice</u> to live in Heaven or Hell. They are <u>not</u> places, (geographic locations.) "...*The kingdom of God cometh not with observations: Neither shall they say, Lo here! or, lo there! for, behold, the kingdom of God is* <u>within</u> *you* " ((Luke 17: 20, 21) Heaven and Hell are states of consciousness which we call into existence through our own attitudes. The Omnipresence of Spirit lives within you and me. Spirit will never leave, condemn, or discipline. It will always be protective, an eternal light, a still small voice. It will make the crooked places straight; It will make dissension disappear and peace abide. When we have faith in the Omnipresence of God, we abide in Heaven. Do we really have anything to lose by stepping out on faith? Even most non-believers know deep within, there is something, some Higher Power at work in the Universe, some Supreme Being.

There is that within us we can liken to a computer, and everyday we push buttons, and program ideas; these condition our lives. There is a button that conditions faith; when we push it, healings of all kind will occur. The faith center opens the mind of the believer, and the more trust activated, the more power manifested.

When you choose to enter into a program of classes, and read inspirational works, share experiences and ideas with others, and begin to meditate daily, you will advance rapidly. Those who hold back will also grow, but at a slower pace. We are always on an upward spiral, and in our growth will hit plateaus that slow us down. How we handle the plateaus depend on how strong our faith is. Our Creator has given to us the gift of choice; we are free to do or as Shakespeare would say, "not to do."

Faith is a great Power and you can prove it works. Bring to mind a simple desire- one that is reasonable, and one you can believe in. Hold it in mind, and see it fulfilled. Know your desire is <u>completed</u> in the ethers/heaven. The knowing, coupled with the certainty *"For where two or three are gathered..."* (Matthew 18:20), will energize your enthusiasm and manifest the desire. This will give you the confirmation that Faith is a Power - a Power to bring forth all your dreams.

Are you a gambler? Do you take chances? I am going to give you another opportunity to prove to yourself that Faith is a Power; however, you must follow the rules. Copy on a 3x5 card the affirmation* below, and place it where you will see it several times a day. I prefer the bathroom mirror; the refrigerator is a good spot also. Read it, memorize it, and repeat it, as often as you can during the day. This is the important part; <u>believe it</u>! Put as much feeling into it as you can muster.

This affirmation will not only firm up your faith in yourself, but you will receive new ideas and thoughts. The ways and means to accomplish your desires will begin to flood your mind. You will see the manifestation beginning to take place. It cannot fail. It will not fail! If you do your part, God will do His. Activate your Power of Faith, use the affirmation, and know your highest and best dreams are being answered - <u>now</u>!

God Bless You.

* Affirmation:
<u>"I am a child of God endowed with the Presence and Power of God within me to help me achieve my every good and great desire."</u>

CHAPTER XI:
STRENGTH

Good Morning!
    Without a doubt, a primal energy pervades the entire universe and fills the vast space. It is not given just to one person or group; it belongs to everyone, and works with everyone-<u>whether it is realized or not</u>. It is Ever-Present and is the Substance in which we live, and move, and have our being. This energy or force is Universal Energy. It is Divine, Everlasting, and All Encompassing. We have named it "God," Jesus called it "Father." Man has mistakenly made It in his image, giving It a form, and in doing so, created separation and limitation. This powerful energy flows and shares its potency with its offspring. One of the attributes (powers) of this energy is strength.

    In the Old Testament, God is referred to as, Jehovah. Metaphysically, Jehovah stands for the "I AM" or "The Christ." This is the seed, the potential, the spiritual nucleus which abides in everyone. Jehovah is forever breathing life into the nostrils of Adam man. Adam man is primarily concerned with all things material; however, deep within he knows there is something more.

    We have within us many different active personalities... the wise, the foolish, the kind, the cruel, the generous, the stingy, the loving, and the hateful. Everyday we come to a cross road in which one personality shows forth more than the other. Jesus proved He overcame the world and the negative personalities in it. He conquered what we think is 'reality.' It is written, *"For now we see through a glass darkly;"* (1 Corinthians 13:12) He mastered the limitation of disease and disability by recognizing that the body in itself does <u>not</u> have power. He knew that all true Power was, and is, from God, the Father, the Great Source of all, the Universal Energy, which gives life.

As Jesus began his ministry, He gathered twelve men. Metaphysically, these twelve represent the Powers inherent in us all. We, too, can call upon, use and gather all the attributes (Powers,) and achieve what Jesus did.

Peter (who represents Faith,) had a brother, Andrew. In the Greek, Andrew means "strong man" and so it is that he is the disciple, which represents strength in man. The qualities of this faculty are durability, stability, and dependability. Man believes strength to be physical prowess; however, that is not the strength I refer to. I am positive that everyone has had a glimpse, or has experienced the strength represented by Andrew. There may have been a time when you needed to be a stabilizing influence for a loved one or for yourself during what appeared to be an unstable condition or traumatic event. Somehow, somewhere, from deep within you, came the strength to get through the ordeal. From deep within the courage came forth, the fortitude to say, to be, to do, whatever was necessary at the time. There are those who embody this Power, and others bury it-assuming it does not exist for them. However, we are the offspring, the image of, the very expression of God. His Power is our gift. It is just waiting for us to call it forth, to rely upon it and use it.

Samson was known for his great strength. Metaphysically, he represents physical strength under Spiritual discipline. Samson, like John, was a Nazarene. This meant they abstained from strong drink and wine; they did not eat meat, would not go near a dead body, and did not cut their hair. Religiously, it meant they were the chosen. They were consecrated to God. The Nazarenes made a vow to give themselves completely to the Lord by giving up all thoughts of worldliness in order to be free from the belief in error. (sin).

The life story of Samson represents different phases of strength in the human consciousness. He was able to perform what appeared to be super human feats because he stayed centered in God. However, when he met Delilah, he temporarily let go of his concentration, and his vow. In a moment of weakness, as he lay sleeping in her lap, she cut off his hair, and he lost his strength. The Philistines were able to overpower him, put out his eyes, and throw him into prison. While there, he realized his mistake and returned to righteous thinking; as his hair began to grow his power returned.

Let us remember, we are talking about spiritual and mental strength. The Bible tells us *"…be strong in the Lord and in the power of his might."* (Ephesians

6:10) In other words, be strong in thought for this establishes a strong mind and body. Do not allow thoughts of weakness to enter into consciousness. We are not subject to physical law but to Spiritual law. Mind is the maker! We are the result of ideas sown and held in mind.

In Jesus' parables, He taught that in sowing seed we reaped a harvest according to the receptivity of the soil. Paul reiterated this by saying, "...*for whatsoever a man soweth, that he shall also reap*" (Galatians 6:7). Seed equals ideas; soil equals mind, receptivity equals a type of soil. Sow positive seed thoughts and receive a bountiful harvest. Sow negative seed thoughts and receive a meager one.

Another familiar and well-known example of strength is the story of David and Goliath. David was a shepherd who trusted in God. He had no fear. Goliath, on the other hand, was a giant, and his power existed principally in his ability to frighten - not unlike any bully today. The Israelites' fear of him, induced by his great size, and his pomp of outer display; led to no one being able to stand up to him. His very presence made them afraid. Goliath, seeing this, was confident that he could fight and win just by his appearance. David, having Spiritual strength and trust, knew his Power came from God. He approached Goliath in a simple and inoffensive manner. He went forth with one idea-to prove there was a God in Israel-the One and Only God. With this in mind, he subdued and prevailed over the giant.

There are many lessons in this story. One such lesson is the conflict between the Spiritual and the worldly with each striving for supremacy in mind. Jesus went through a time of indecision when tempted by the 'devil.' He could have used His God given Powers to become a worldly king, but He knew that His mission was to bring Love and Truth to man. He made His choice and put "satan," the voice that seeks human gratification, behind Him. When we do not realize the Spiritual Truth that governs worldly manifestation, it is easy to get lost in the pomp and power of the outside world. To overcome the world is simple, not easy, but simple. In meeting any and all challenges, have the knowledge "I am a child of God," and know that with God as your partner, all adverse appearance can be changed. In life, we get so caught up in "making mountains out of molehills," that when things happen, and challenges occur in and around us, (our Goliath), we forget this too shall pass. Through the Power of love, and the assurance that God is active in our lives, it is possible to subdue any challenges that occur. There is One Power and One Presence in the Universe and It is in charge. Always!

Everyone uses the Power; anyone can become lost and misdirect it. It says in Deuteronomy "*…to love the Lord your God, and to serve Him with all your heart and with all your soul.*" (11:13) I have heard it said that only a selfish God would ask such a thing. As a parent, are you selfish in asking your child to obey? We ask for obedience to keep them from harm, and so it is with our Parent. Within us is a Power to do, be, and create. It is always there constantly working and giving direction.

It is possible to become confused, and it is difficult to remain single-minded. We fall easily into the trap of blaming someone or something else when we become sad, hurt, and angry. In doing so, we give our Power over to another. Why? First, we run from accepting self-responsibility; we are afraid to admit what is going on in our minds. Secondly, and this is hard to accept, no one has the power to hurt or harm us <u>unless we allow it</u>! When we accept the hurt, (get angry; strike back), we give our Power to another. We do this because secretly, deep within, we agree with what has been said or done. We become defensive to protect ourselves. When we strike back, and deliberately create sadness, or perpetuate anger, we are acting out "emotionally." These feelings belong to the manifest world of our making, and we are not of this world. We are Spiritual beings, living in a Spiritual world, governed by Spiritual law, created by our Spiritual Father.

Jesus knew! Jesus taught that the thoughts and prayers we hold in mind have already been accomplished. When He prayed, He thanked the Father knowing it was done! When He raised Lazarus, His exact words were, "*Father, I thank Thee that you hast heard me. And I knew that you hearest me always:*" (John 11: 41, 42) He had no doubt that He was heard, that God would provide. He had no doubt His prayer would be granted. Jesus, confident with the strength of conviction, knew whatever and whenever He asked, it would be done!

Ironically, we do not understand that it is our <u>fear</u> of certain conditions, or diseases, and that by <u>dwelling</u> on them or putting a label (name) to them, <u>we are bringing those fears into full expression.</u> We do not realize our Power, but know this <u>Thoughts Held in Mind Create After Their Kind</u>. It may be more difficult to declare the good in one's life, <u>regardless of appearance</u>, than to hold fearfully onto dreaded assumptions, but the results are far more joyous. Sadly, it seems as if we relish hearing and believing in the worst gossip and scenarios instead of the cheerful. I personally believe it is because most of us have been raised hearing, "*...man, that is a worm?... and the son of man, which is a worm*" (Job 25:6). This sets the stage for us to begin life with a low opinion of who and what we are. When in Truth, "*...Ye are the sons of the living God.*" (Hosea 1:10) As God's child, we are given dominion over the manifest world. "*And God said,... and let them have dominion over...all the earth,...*" (Genesis 1:26) and in verse 28: "*...and over every living thing...*" God, the Creator, our Father-Mother made us co-creators with Him. He created love; we have created fear.

True Strength comes from within. It takes strength to affirm who and what we are. It takes more strength to live it. Once we begin to put forth the effort all the Powers will come together to work with us in order that we may be what we truly are-a Divine child of Loving God.

The blessings of Strength are many: they give freedom from weakness, stability of character, power to withstand temptation, and the ability to accomplish the goals we set in life. This is your legacy. It is up to you to use it. What do you have to lose?

God Bless.

* Dear reader, if you harbor any thought at all that the world, and its conditions have control over you such as, "you can't fight city hall," then what harm could there be in accepting the opposite to be true. Hold these thoughts in mind, <u>"There is One Presence and One Power in the universe, God, and He cannot fail."</u> <u>"I am an expression of God!"</u> I promise, if you try, you will discover the many blessings God is ready to impart to you.

CHAPTER XII:
YOUR INHERENT JUDGMENT

Good Morning!

In the Bible, there are three disciples mentioned more than the others; they are Peter (Faith), John (Love), and James, who is the disciple who represents Judgment. Metaphysically, each represents an essential Power or attribute that work together to establish a well-balanced individual. Judgment is the ability to discern <u>rightfully</u>. It gives us the power to evaluate and make good decisions as well as make the right choices for others and ourselves. When we use all three spiritually - in other words, when we love unconditionally, have faith in God only, and judge righteously without malice - life takes on a special meaning.

One of the twelve Powers (faculties-abilities) that man has within, which is an inherent gift from his Creator, is Judgment; this also includes Wisdom. The way in which we use this Power depends on our understanding and awareness, or our closeness to our God-self. When we become aware of who we truly are-Spiritual beings-a light begins to dawn within, and there is a quickening of our Judgment faculty. We begin to doubt the validity of previous thoughts and teachings. We begin to see with an inner eye. We begin to view our fellowman and events from a new understanding.

For a long time, many scorned and said that intuition was flimsy and weak. It was always associated with emotional women. Most of us have those feelings but are afraid to trust them while others, having the same feelings, have used them and discovered they are accurate.

Spiritual discernment is a quick knowing, an automatic realization of the truth in a situation. Intuition, Judgment, Wisdom, Discernment, are all-natural to us and belong to us through Divine Sonship. Did not Jesus the Christ proclaim, "...*Is it not written in your law, I said, Ye are gods?*" (John

10:34) Within us is a Wisdom that is pure and peaceable, and if we hold steadily to the guidance within, we will soon discover that our standards of right and wrong will undergo rapid changes.

Some are unaware, or doubt, that there are numerous laws of justice for the highest good of all. One is <u>Karma</u>. To put it in layman's terms, "what goes around comes around." To quote Biblical law, *"For with what judgment ye judge, ye shall be judged: and with what measure ye mete, it shall be measured to you again."* (Matthew 7: 2)

The laws of the Universe, both great and small, work for us continually. We did not make the laws; they are God's Laws! He established them for our use and our good before the forming of the world. Jesus did not discover anything new; He was neither the first nor the last to make use of the law of health. When He healed, He simply called wholeness into expression by seeing it in those who could not see it for themselves. He cleansed their minds and opened them to the reality of who they personified - their creator, God!

Those of us in Unity are familiar with the counsel, "Let Go and Let God." These are words of wisdom, which bring release from fear - from the ills of the outer world, and from our own individual worlds. The suffering that we put ourselves through relates to the misuse of the Judgment faculty. Many times during the day, we bring suffering to ourselves, not because of <u>a</u> fact, but because of our 'opinion' or judgment <u>of</u> the fact.

Everyone is familiar with the proverbs, "Let sleeping dogs lie;" "Don't cry over spilt milk." Although we know them, we do not realize what practical and useful tools they are in everyday living. When Socrates lay dying, he said to his friends, "I bid you think of Truth and not of Socrates." Along those same lines, Emmet Fox wrote a book, *The Golden Key*. It contains the message that when your feelings are hurt, when you are experiencing loss, or when you are in the midst of trouble, when anxiety and worry are bogging you down, think of Truth. Think of God. He emphasized that when challenged take your mind off the problem and replace it with thoughts of good.

The mind has a way of magnifying what it looks upon. When challenges occur, we grab hold of the problem, and the negative condition grows all out of proportion. We are then in a world of anguish, turmoil, and despair. If we can learn to turn away from the problem, it begins to diminish for the mind cannot hold two diverse thoughts at once. *"…choose you this day whom you will serve…as for me and my house, we will serve the lord."* (Joshua 24:15) To serve 'a devil' (if you believe in one) is to dwell on the problem; to serve God is to release, let go, knowing He will aid you. This returns us to a state of harmony and a knowing that all will be well.

Before we ask our Creator for anything, we must 'forgive.' I do not know how you define forgiveness, but I had the idea that it was an act of being magnanimous; in some ways even patronizing, for example, to say, "It's O.K. I forgive <u>you</u>;" would be a way to make me appear the better person. Emily Cady, the author of *Lessons in Truth*, Unity's textbook, defines forgiveness as a giving - giving love for hate, understanding for misunderstanding, and tolerance for intolerance.

I have always believed that no one can make you feel or do anything that you do not wish to feel or do. I believe nothing external, no outside physical presence, has any power to hurt, make me sick or afraid, not only me, but anyone, unless we <u>allow it by agreement</u>. All dominion, all power, lies within each individual. We may very well question this but if we really search our souls, we come to understand it is our own deep feelings of being inadequate that make us want to strike back.

Just what does this have to do with forgiveness and judgment? Each one of us lives in a world of our own making. It is a world created from ideas, beliefs, and judgments observed by us and taught to us as we were growing up. We continue to form new ideas and beliefs during our lifetime. We rely on them and they become our truth. We see a situation and according to our rules, our ideas of right and wrong, we pass judgment. We meet people and form our opinion of them according to what we see through our eyes and interpret through hearing. This interpretation of what we see and hear we place in our minds into a category of right and wrong. These perceptions are in accord with our individual beliefs.

We all seek approval, we all look for love and everyone wants respect. What we fail to see is that approval, love, and respect may mean different things to different people. Too often, a word said can cut to the quick, and the person who said it is an unsuspecting attacker. We suffer not because of what a person has said but how we have interpreted it. That interpretation is judgment.

I do not believe in a devil. I do not believe in a man with a pitchfork and a tail. I do not believe in an outside power greater than the Spirit of God within me. What I do believe is that there is another part of me that fights for rule, it is subtle, corrupt, tenacious, and, oh, so justifiable. The name of that part of me is 'ego'. There are two pathways in life we may walk. We can surrender to a Higher Self, which is All-Good, All-Knowing, All-Loving. It will guide and keep us safe, It will lead us to a realm of peace and fulfillment, It will lead us to joy and happiness.

The other pathway is to allow the ego, which gives the illusion of one being in complete control that has full sway. Ironically, those who believe they are in charge of their own lives are the ones that cry out that they cannot control world conditions, circumstances, or events that appear to attack them. This is one of the subtleties of the ego It places blame on outer conditions or other people never taking self-responsibility. When we become fearful, hurt, or angry, we think, "someone is attacking me"; we feel an enemy is invading our world trying to take something from us, whether it be approval, love, or respect, and we retaliate. Beloved of God, this is a false premise. You already are love; you were created in love as love. You already have the approval and respect of your Father-Mother God for God sees only the good that you are and do.

Yes, I will admit to you there are those people that we meet that are cruel and rude. They hurt inside, for some reason or other, and want to lash out. They feel justified hurting others. They do cross our paths, but why do we allow them to hurt us? The answer is because of our own expectations. We expect people to act in a certain way, usually in the same way that we have been programmed which is the way we have been brought up to believe and accept is the proper way to act. However, my way is not necessarily your way. The more we hold on to ideas of right and wrong, the more we judge. That is why Jesus said, "*But I say unto you, That ye resist not evil: but whosoever shall smite thee on thy right cheek, turn to him the other also.*" (Matthew 5:39) He cautions us not to "take to heart" words or deeds, but turn away, recognize and know there is no right or wrong. <u>Things just are!</u>

It is a matter of letting go, forgiving, letting go the hurt for peace of mind. It is important to learn to walk away from disagreement and disappointments because a person who continues to feel hurt, unloved, and/or unpopular develops an attitude of defeat and failure.

There are those who say they want happiness while carrying around with them the air of gloom and sadness. They find no satisfaction in life. They feel nothing will turn out right for them. This kind of thinking is destructive.

It is our attitude about life that determines the world we live in, not the circumstances.

A judgment is a settled opinion, a fixed view of things. This kind of judgment will put a person in his own private prison, and the guard standing by will be ego.

God has given us a gift, and that gift is the seed of perfection, the Christ within. We all have some definition of God, and Jesus the Christ, but we are vague about the Holy Spirit. We describe the ego as personality, the face we show the world, the voice inside our head, which is selfish, and out for number one. You know the message, "Think of yourself because if you don't no one else will;" This voice tells us to believe <u>only</u> in what can be determined as true through our senses. Once we understand what the ego is, then we can define the Holy Spirit. The Holy Spirit is the still small voice that God uses to communicate with us; the voice that will guide us to our highest good-<u>if we will listen</u>. The Holy Spirit can help one to diminish the ego's hold. The Holy Spirit will correct judgment. Where there was hurt and anger, there will be peace and love. There is no need for forgiveness in the eyes of the Holy Spirit because there is no error to forgive. The need for forgiveness is for <u>us</u> as individuals to help cleanse <u>our</u> souls, <u>our</u> consciousness, and <u>our</u> attitudes. Once we release and allow this action to take over, we begin to feel the freedom of love. A mind always on the defensive is primed to attack and cannot know love.

The first step in healing is learning to let go. Believe me; I know how difficult this can be. However, when something hurtful is done or said to us, <u>if</u> it is not released, resentment sets in. To resent means to be angry; when we are angry, we go over and over the situation; we relive it, and keep it alive in consciousness. This affects our attitude. This causes stress, which can lead to health problems. Everyone has made mistakes, erred in action, and said hurtful things. We have disappointed others, ourselves included, and been defeated, but it is not the end of the world. The individual failures do not matter. What matters is the progress we make as we learn to overcome. The Chinese have a saying, "The fault is not in falling down, it is in lying there."

Poor judgment causes problems. It makes us critical, it makes us angry, and at times, it may even give us a feeling of superiority. One thing I believe-it will always create for us a hell on earth.

We use righteous Judgment when we raise our consciousness to a place where there is no critique, to a place of acceptance. This comes from an understanding that as children of God, we are equal and are entitled to be and do, as individual conscious directs, even if it is in complete opposition from our own viewpoint. Remember life is a school, and we advance, or fall behind, at our own rate of learning. Acceptance is our gateway to heaven.

You do not have to take my word for it. Try it for yourself. The next time someone says something hurtful to you, as soon as you feel those feelings of anger and retaliation begin; do not try to justify your anger by defiling the other's character. Instead, take a moment to stop and recognize this individual is in a bad space and has a need to lash out. Unfortunately, you got into his space. Agree with your adversary. Do not judge the whys and wherefores, but try understanding through forgiveness. Dear one, you are a Spiritual being - God's offspring. Your adversary is also God's offspring - your brother. Your brother is hurting because he is listening to his ego. You have the opportunity to listen to the Holy Spirit. The power lies within you.

We hear so much about Judgment Day. In Truth, every day is Judgment day. We have the gift of choice. We choose how/what to think about others and situations daily. It is up to us to choose what is worthwhile, loving, and peaceable, to be positive in the midst of mayhem. We have the Power to bring forth the highest good, not only for ourselves but also for others. *"Chose you this day whom ye will serve."* (Joshua 24:15)

God Bless, Know He Loves You!

CHAPTER XIII:
Love Is a Power

Good Morning!

There is a simple song in our hymnals, "Love is the only power, Love is the only way..." Since this is the month we set aside to honor love, I decided to take this opportunity to speak about another of our innate Powers. I feel it is appropriate at this time to delve deeper into this faculty in order to have a better understanding of it.

Paul wrote that love is the greatest of all things for when we have love of self, love of fellowman, love of the world, and love of life itself, we have peace. The disciple, John, represents love. He was the youngest disciple, and the brother of James, who represents, Judgment. We are speaking today of pure love, the love expressed, and guided by Divine Mind; this is what John represents. A love that knows it is one with mankind, a love which gives unselfishly, a love which desires only good for everyone.

There is an implication that God's Love is fickle; He can give it, and take it away. That is a <u>misconception</u>. God does not Love anyone; God <u>is</u> the love <u>in</u> everyone. God does not, and will not, push any of His attributes on us. They are His gifts for us to use. We were given free will-it is up to us to discern the Truth of His gifts, and how/if we will apply them. This we do by word and deed - especially by deed. For is it not true that actions speak louder than words? We are created equal with the same powers, the same abilities, the same Divine potential, and it is through our searching, our desire, and our own understanding, that we bring forth our true nature.

Our first experience with love is in infancy. We sense it from the care given to us by our parents. We come to know physical love, as we grow older, by holding onto them with our arms around their neck, or clasping their hand. We even discovered love for things as we held tenaciously to a favorite toy; our learning of love continued throughout the years centering on self, the ego self.

In order to learn and share pure Love, unconditional Love, it is important that we learn to love ourselves. If I were to ask any of you here this morning, "Do you love yourself?" the answer, in all probability would be a resounding "yes!" However, buried down deep in the recesses of your being may be thoughts of unworthiness, frustration, unfulfilled desires because the confidence that true Self-Love gives is missing.

Love in Divine Mind is the idea of Universal unity! It is the Power that attracts and brings people together; it aligns all things, and allows Spirit to flow freely. When we fall in love, we feel as if we were on top of the world. It is this feeling that stabilizes our circulation and makes us feel healthy and happy. Mentally, Love will harmonize the thoughts in your mind. Love is a Spiritual faculty expressed primarily as a feeling. When we feel at one with someone, "we are sharing Love." When we desire good in the lives of those around us, "we are sharing Love." It is in this sharing that we have a sense of belonging, a sense of unity.

We limit love when we personalize it. By that I mean, we center it on the things closest to us, and in some circumstances, we become so attached to our loved ones it may border on the edge of obsession. We confine our love to "only" family and friends. In this way, we separate ourselves from God's true meaning of Love. Love should include everyone. *"A new commandment I give unto you, That ye love one another; as I have loved you, that ye also love one another."* (John 13:34) Can you possibly imagine God or Jesus centering Their Love <u>only</u> on certain or close individuals?

There are many basics to Love; one is patience - the patience to wait and know that all things are working together for good no matter what the appearance. When there is a misunderstanding in the home, whether it is with a spouse, or child, patient Love has a calming effect. It soothes and grants us the tolerance to listen. Every day, we have many opportunities to exercise patience. From the time we arise until we go to bed, we are in contact with loved ones, friends, acquaintances, and strangers, all capable of pushing our buttons. If we truly desire to be on the Spiritual path, we have the Power, within to call upon our faculty of Love to see us through the day.

Kindness is another form of Love. It is showing someone you care. It can be a simple, "Thank You," or given in a more time consuming act of ministering to someone who is ill. It can be paying attention to someone who needs a little attention, or just listening to someone who wants to talk. We never know what effect our kindness will have on another. Let me illustrate with this story:

A traveling salesman was hurriedly passing through a railroad station when he saw a crippled beggar sitting with his pencils and a cup. He dropped a coin into his cup as he passed by. After a few steps, he stopped, and wondered about his action, he returned to the man and said, "I want to apologize to you, I treated you like a beggar, and you are really a merchant." He then stooped and took a pencil.

Two years later, the same salesman was rushing through the station and a voice called, "Hey, Mister," he turned, and there was the same crippled man. This time however, he was sitting on a high stool working as a proprietor of a busy newsstand. He said, "You may not remember me but I will never forget you. You treated me as a person, and for the first time in my life, I realized I could make something of myself. I have found a way to be self-supporting, but most of all I now have my self-respect."

It only takes a minute to change the path of another's life with a simple kindness, that kindness - a form of Love.

Then there is generosity - the act of giving in all aspects of our lives. When we are generous, there is no thought of envy or jealousy. It is an opening of our hearts, and giving forth purely for the sake of giving. There is no thought of "having to" or duty. There is no other motive or intention; it is an act of love.

Humility is an aspect of Love in which one discerns, "we are all brothers." There is no such thing as one person being better than another, of one being more important than another, or of one deserving more than another.

Being courteous is another aspect of kindness, and shows that we are thinking of the good of someone else. Unselfishness is to give completely and happily, not for what it will do for us, but for the joy it gives to another. When someone holds his temper, and thinks twice before lashing out and saying or doing something that may cause harm, that is another form of love. Words spoken in haste are a boomerang which have a way of coming back to attack.

To be guileless is to eradicate deceitful and hurtful thoughts. In other words, think no evil. It is not possible to show love to our fellow man when we try to deceive by thinking or speaking lies about him/her.

Sincerity, to look into someone's eyes, and to say, in complete honesty, "I love you," fills one with a warmth that courses throughout the entire body. We do this easily to close family; but what about friends and acquaintances? I know it would be presumptuous to walk up to a stranger or adversary and say it, but there is nothing to stop us from thinking it.

One of the most joyous, and beautiful experiences I have had was at Unity Village. During a class, we were singing Joy songs, and the instructor asked us to get a partner, form a circle; and then turn and face our partner. The next task was hard. She said we were to look deep into the person's eyes, and with all the feeling we could muster, say, "I love you" and then move on to the next person. I say it was hard because there were some "strangers" in the class, and I, at times, am shy.

I know people who have no difficulty in showing emotion, and some who find it extremely hard to do. Such a mixture was in that group. Hesitantly, we began. As we went around the room, the vibrations began to set in, and the feelings became heightened. It became such a moving experience that when we were done, there were tears in most of the classmates' eyes.

We have the Meet and Greet part of the Unity service where we mingle and hug each other. Some put their hands out to shake instead of giving a hug. They are shy and reserved, but once that shyness is overcome, and they can lose their inhibitions, they come to understand and receive a glimpse of what "God is Love" means. There is a reason for the hugs. It is learning to become open to the experience of sharing a bit of yourself with another, to achieve a feeling of oneness - of unity. Love is more than affection; it is more than sex. It is an inner current, which is real and has substance. Love is a force that will solidify and heal.

There are certain words that when used repeatedly can transform conditions of the mind, body and affairs. You do not have to take my word for it; you can experience it for yourself. If you were to read the Thirteenth Chapter of Corinthians once a week for three months, it would change your life forever.

It appears as if no one takes into account the difference between Divine Love and human love. Divine Love is broad, and takes in the Universe, and everything within it. It is accepting, it is understanding, and, most of all, forgiving. Divine love will establish fearlessness, courage, and sets us free from negative situations. Human love is fickle, selfish, and confining. Human love exists in fear.

We are one with God through the Spirit of the Christ. There is a potential, a seed within man, and that seed is the Only Begotten Son of God. It is The Christ! In order to have the same mind in you that was/is in Jesus the Christ, we must learn to think and believe as He did. We accomplished this by calling upon the twelve Faculties/Powers to help us.

The word 'breath' in the Bible is the symbol for inspiration. Jesus breathed upon the disciples and said, *"receive ye the Holy Ghost:"* (John 20:22) The more we work to bring forth the twelve Powers, the closer we come to achieving the Spiritual Identity that is ours by Divine Right.

In an earlier talk, I stated that faith is building a firm foundation. It is holding fast to the Truth of God and His Goodness, to His Love for us. In doing so, we breathe life into our belief system. Unconditional Love has to be cultivated. Unless we are free of grudges, resentments, and envies of any kind, we cannot show forth Love in its fullest expression. Realization of the Omnipotence, (all power,) Omniscience, (all knowledge,) and the Omnipresence, (the Presence of God, always, everywhere present,) will free you from fearful emotions that may beset you. Test yourself today. At the first sign of an unloving situation, ask yourself, "Why is this upsetting me? What feeling/memory is this bringing up? Am I being resentful? Is it jealousy?" The answers will come - from a book, from a friend, or even sometimes as an inner knowing. Acceptance of the answer may prove difficult. We as human beings may claim to accept self-responsibility, but in reality, we run from it. It is so much easier to blame someone or something else when things go wrong. When the answer comes, think of your Creator. Stand apart from the situation and fill yourself with the Presence and Power of the Love, which dwells within. The situation will change. If by any chance you do not see immediate results, just wait. I guarantee they will be forthcoming. Have faith! True Love casts out <u>so-called</u> evil because Love, itself sees no evil.

Once a year on Valentines Day, we set aside a day for loved ones. I suggest you set this day aside for those in your life you feel you cannot love - those who have upset you, those who have caused discontent, whether at home or at the office. You need only to think of the person and mentally forgive them.

If it is a long-standing grudge, it may take some time to come to terms with this idea; however, for your own good make the effort to make amends.

When we were kids, we heard the chant, "Sticks and stones may break my bones, but names will never harm me." Unfortunately, this is not true. The name shouted at us, does influence us as we go through life. Why is this so? Believe it or not when we hear disparaging remarks, we secretly agree. Otherwise, it would be a simple thing to say, "That is what you think but I know better."

It has nothing to do with the other person's slander; it does its damage because we bury the words, and hold them in memory. For example, if someone called you fat, and in reality, you felt good about your weight, you would come back with a comment, walk off and forget it. However, if you believed you were overweight, and were uncomfortable with the way you looked, your anger would soar, and the hurt would sink into your subconscious mind. Left there to fester, years later if anyone says anything relating to your looks or body that old memory returns, and the desire to lash out rears up. Therefore, you see, dear ones, sticks and stones can cause harm because we have the power to agree, or discard, to love or hate. It is a Truth <u>no</u> one has the power to hurt or harm us <u>without</u> our permission. We have the power of choice and can master whatever feelings we wish to live with.

Let me ask you, do you want to be resentful and accept someone else's misconception of you, or do you want to be at peace?

Every Loving thought, word, or deed that you do, becomes part of the Universal Consciousness, which strengthens and brings a new awareness to mankind. As the offspring of God, it is our responsibility to work diligently at being an expression of Love. The rewards are many.

I will leave you this morning with one thought. It is a Bible scripture that you can use as an affirmation to extinguish the feelings of hate. I urge you to use it freely and often.

"*Beloved, let us love one another: for love is of God.*" (1 John 4:7)

Have a Love filled Day!

CHAPTER XIV:
Imagination Is a Gift

Good Morning!

Once upon a time, there lived a prince with a crooked back. One day he summoned a sculptor and asked him to fashion a statue of himself, an exact likeness, except with a straight back. The prince told him, "I wish to see myself as I might have been." When the statue was completed, the prince looked at it daily; he admired it and studied it. Days, weeks, and months went by and a rumor began to circulate throughout the kingdom, "The prince's back was straight." And behold it was true! (A Fable)

Charles Fillmore, co-founder of Unity, wrote in *Keep a True Lent,* "God's greatest gift to man is the power of thought, through which he can incorporate into his consciousness, the Mind of God." (p.147) It is through the power of thought, we mold our lives; it is through the power of thought, we attract to us our good; it is through the power of thought, we know who and what we are - Spiritual beings made in the image and likeness of God. Can you realize the significance of this? We have the ability, as God's offspring, to bring forth into manifestation whatever we picture in mind. Our imagination gives us the ability to visualize and demonstrate. Imagination gives form to ideas.

The disciple Bartholomew, a friend of Phillip's, represents the Imagination. (In John 1:45-49 he was called Nathanael, it is thought that Bartholomew was Nathanael's surname.) As reported when Jesus was gathering the disciples together, He 'saw' Bartholomew under a fig tree, "a long way off," discerning his presence before reaching him. It is through this faculty-this power of imaging that we are able-with our minds eye to see mental pictures that bring forth and give form to things in the outer.

Big business gives special seminars and workshops to their employees that emphasize goal setting. There are many self-help books written on how to improve one's life using the same techniques. Unity has been teaching this method of self-accomplishment for over one hundred years. We call it The Power of your Imagination.

An instructor at a seminar will say, "You must have goals in your life. Begin by deciding what you want in the years ahead. Is it to be a successful business man/woman, an accountant, doctor, or lawyer? Look ahead to what you want to accomplish with your life; do you desire a career only, or a home, marriage, and family? Unity teaches, "<u>See</u> yourself as a successful business man, accountant, doctor, lawyer. If so desired, <u>see</u> yourself as married in five years, and starting a family in seven." The class instructor calls it goal setting; Unity calls it Imaging.

Setting a goal is stating a desire - picturing the fulfillment of that desire is imaging. In the story of Pinocchio, Jiminy Cricket tells him "Wishing will make it so." It matters not whether one has a dream, sets a goal, or makes a wish, each one calls upon the Power of Imagination.

We are always thinking, and thoughts bring with it pictures. Regrettably, few realize this power works not only with positive thoughts but with negative ones also. Jesus said, "*Ye are the light of the world.*" (Matthew 5:14) "*Let your light so shine before men, that they may see your good works, and glorify your Father which is in heaven,*" (Matthew 5:16) He is telling us to know the Truth of Oneness, know the Power within, know God is Love, Life and Wholeness. Live it. Be it. Be the living proof that you are the off-spring of God who is your Creator. However, Jesus knew his fellow man thus he also said, "*…that light is come into the world, and men loved darkness rather than light,…*" (John 3:19)

Is it not true? We love gossip, and the more negative, the more we digest it. Maybe it is a self-preservation technique, "if this is happening to so and so then it won't happen to me," kind of thinking. I think this is a possibility because we see through human eyes rather than Spiritual ones. Do we not contend, "Seeing is believing?" Haven't we heard that since we were knee high to a grasshopper? Do we not judge what is right and/or wrong by what is right in front of us; do we not judge 'reality' by what we hear/and read? Ah! That is the rub. Let me explain:

We read in the newspaper, the economy is bad, then we 'see in mind" limited conditions.

We hear the flu season is upon us and 'see ourselves' coughing and sneezing with chills and fever.

Senior citizens hear there will be a social security cut, and see themselves destitute, hungry, and afraid.

A patient hears the doctor pronounce a dreaded diagnosis, and imagines he is growing weaker, and begins to anticipate horrible pain.

Yes, I agree with Papa Charles-imagination is a gift, and all of God's gifts are meant for good. Unfortunately, we humans have a way of distorting His gifts. Whatever one sees in mind, whatever one imagines their world to be, will be! Like begets like, as a man thinketh in his heart, (soul), so it is!

I dare you to begin right now to use your imagination to turn your world around. Whatever your lack, whatever your challenge, whatever your need, it can be changed to prosperity, opportunity, and fulfillment through the renewing of your mind.

We are special! We are great! We are unique because <u>we are Spiritual Beings</u>, living in a Spiritual World, governed by Spiritual Law. Spiritual Law supersedes man's law. It is written, "*Ye are of God, little children,......greater is He that is in you, than he that is in the world.*" (1 John 4:4)

There is nothing new about using one's imagination. Prehistoric man carved pictures of the food he desired, believing an unseen power would attract to him what was pictured.

During the Golden Age of Greece, the Greeks surrounded pregnant women with pictures and statues that were lovely to look at. They believed the unborn child would receive the pictures, <u>via the mother's mind</u>, and be born healthy and beautiful. When I was a child, this idea still prevailed and I knew several ethnic families that would not allow anything negative or ugly said around a pregnant woman for fear of scarring her unborn child.

It is a Truth. <u>Thoughts held in mind create after their kind</u> and it is through the imagination that we draw to ourselves whatever we hold in consciousness. This may sound like an old wives tale, protecting mothers-to-be, and I am not saying that someone who looks upon "ugly' or 'distorted' pictures will produce ugly babies. I am saying, we do manifest in our lives what we <u>believe</u> to be <u>true</u>, and as long as pregnant women know- in their hearts their little ones are safe, it will be!

We must remember, fifty, one hundred, two hundred years ago, people were very superstitious, and had some fearsome ideas that they believed without question. Therefore, they had negative results. Thankfully, we have come of an age where we realize positive thinking brings more joy. We are overcoming practices of old. We are coming of age into a new understanding which is - it is our own thinking that creates and dominates our world. Whether we recognize it or not, this is a fact.

I am sorry to say when trouble appears on the horizon even those taught Unity teachings forget this Law of the Universe. For example, a young woman (we will call her Ann) begins her Spiritual climb, and learns she is indeed, one with God. Created by Spirit, she is a Spiritual being, and can achieve whatsoever is her desire. Ann begins working on her consciousness to improve herself. She desires to be prosperous. She meditates faithfully and knowingly using affirmations one of which is "I am prospered for God is Good. He is my abundant supplier." She begins tithing, and before long gets a promotion at work with a salary increase. Over time, things get easier and she notices the flow of abundance gradually escalating. She is elated. Then one day she goes for a physical. The doctor finds a small cyst and wants to do a biopsy. I venture to guess Ann listens to the doctor's loud voice ringing in her head and hears the dreaded word, even though he may not have said it. She remembers her relatives telling her about Aunt Helen and Cousin Matilda who died from similar conditions, and the pictures in her head are all doom and gloom. Gone is the reality of her Oneness with God. Gone is the knowing she is a Spiritual being. All that is left is fear, and the images of what "could" be growing larger and more menacing with every passing hour.

Why is it we can see and trust God in one situation, and then forget Him when we need him most? We can visualize more money, but not perfect health. God is our very life, our wholeness, nothing is impossible with Him! There is no such thing as illness- only absence of wholeness. That wholeness comes forth with the power of the imagination. Health can be realized when we hold in mind true positive thoughts. When we see ourselves as one with God, when we accept our true heritage, when we accept our relationship with our brother, Jesus, and hear his words: "*Verily, verily, I say unto you, He that believeth on me, the works that I do shall he do also; and greater works than these shall he do...*" (John 14:12), healing can occur.

What would you like to see in your life? Vision it; use your imagination to bring it forth "*on earth as it is in heaven.*"(in the manifest world as it is in the invisible reign) Begin today to change what you do not want, and bring forth what you do.

Do I hear someone saying I do not have an imagination? Sure you do. You were born with it. It may be you have not made conscious use of it, but it is within you as one of your God-given Powers. Goethe, a well-known philosopher said,

> "If you want to develop a keener appreciation of art, hang a beautiful picture on the wall in a much used area, seeing it consciously, and subconsciously, as you pass by, your ability to see beauty will be raised to a higher degree."

The same holds true for your imagination. Cultivate the habit of seeing, not with your human eyes, but your spiritual eyes; seeing with your human eyes causes every fear known to man. This is the wrong use of imagination for it builds up frightening pictures of suspicion, jealousy, resentment, and self-pity. Seeing through your spiritual eyes, one sees love, acceptance, forgiveness, and wholeness.

Imagination does not work alone. I need to impress upon you it is necessary to have faith while imaging. You can image a full wallet, a healthy body, a loving relationship, "till the cows come home," but if you do <u>not believe in your heart</u>, that it <u>will be</u>, not just possible, but "Be," it will not materialize.

When Jesus healed the man who had been blind since birth, He made a clay pack with his spittle and placed it over the man's eyes. He told him to go to the pool of Siloam where he was to wash his eyes, and once washed, he would see. Now why do you suppose He just did not place His hands on the man and say, "You are healed"? Because Jesus wanted the man to believe, to have faith, to know it was possible. As the man walked to the pool, he would be thinking, "When I wash the clay from my eyes, I will see." That thought would bolster his faith, and using his imaging power would bring about the miracle. It is written, *"According to your faith be it unto you."* (Matthew 9:29)

When you have a creative idea, asleep or awake, on the phone, or from a book, if the idea feels right, albeit it sounds impossible, give credence to the idea that "it came from God." This being the case, you must succeed because all things with God are possible.

In my enthusiasm to make a point, I sometimes repeat myself so if you have heard this story before, please bear with me.

I had been searching; seeking something in my life, I knew not what. Then a friend took me to a Unity church, and as I sat there listening to a 'woman minister' a voice in my head said, "That's what you should do." To be honest, I did not give credence to the voice. It was a crazy idea, or so I thought, but it would not let me go and grew stronger with each passing week. There is another teaching in the healing of the blind man. Things do not happen overnight. Some ideas take time to manifest, (illustrated by the blind man's walk to the pool). It took five years from the time I heard the voice until I was doing the work as a Licensed Unity Teacher, and another five before I was Licensed a Minister and ordained the following year. Once I finally accepted the possibility of the idea and began to work towards it, mentally and physically, what I originally thought to be an impossible feat, I was able to accomplish.

Before I leave you this morning, I would like you to listen to what the psalmist said,

> *"What is man, that thou art mindful of him? and the son of man, that thou visiteth him? For thou hast made him a little lower than the angels, and hast crowned him with glory and honor Thou madest him to have dominion over the works of thy hands: thou hast put all things under his feet: All sheep and oxen; yea, and the beasts of the field; The fowl of the air, and the fish of the sea, and whatsoever passeth through the paths of the seas. Oh, Lord, our Lord. how excellent is thy name in all the earth!"*
>
> (Psalm 8:4-9)

There you have it. How <u>wondrous</u> you are. <u>You</u>, dear one, have dominion. Paul tells us to be transformed by the renewing of the mind. If you are holding pictures of lack, and limitation in your head, you have the power within to change them to abundance and freedom. If you see a sick body, you can change what you see to a healthy one. You have the Power for you are the very image and likeness of your Father-Mother God that gives life to all.

"...*Awake thou that sleepeth,...*" (Ephesians 5:14) Know the Truth. The Omnipresent Spirit of God is forever working in and through every one of his children to manifest more good. We need only to let go, and allow it to happen. It is up to us. We can intentionally use our imagination for good or unknowingly for naught. We have the Power. Why not use it?

Addendum for my readers:

I wish to emphasize to those who may be facing a health challenge, I am not advocating that one should not take/follow medical advice. I believe in Spiritual healing; however, for it to occur, the person who has a challenge <u>must believe</u> in it wholeheartedly, must have <u>complete faith in God</u>.

Always follow your own instincts, your own heart. God gave us free will and because of that, you must make your <u>own decision</u> according to <u>your</u> inner guide. Whether the healing occurs through a physician or Spirit, it is still your own belief system that will bring it forth.

God bless you all!

CHAPTER XV:
Wherein Lies the Power

Good Morning to you!

Have you ever had a friend ask you, "What on the world does the term 'divinity in man' or mind' is the maker' mean?" Following your explanation, the reaction is one of incredulity-associated with a look, which implies you have a screw loose. They laughed at Columbus for his idea that the world was round. How about the Wright Brothers who insisted they could fly? Then there was Thomas Edison who said he could make a 'talking machine'; each one was thought to be absurd. We, in Unity, sometimes receive the same reaction when we try to explain our beliefs and faith. The founders of Unity, Charles and Myrtle Fillmore, based this Spiritual movement completely on the teachings of Jesus the Christ, and discovered, as well as proved His teaching, 'Life is Consciousness.'

In 1720, the Black Death Plague hit Europe. The Spanish clergy said it was the result of attending the opera. The English bishops blamed it on the theater. Some of the clergy took the position it was the fashionable long-pointed shoes, of that day, which infuriated God, and that was the cause. Still others insisted the plague was a direct result of corruption in politics.

We laugh at the 'diagnoses' of the Black plague for we have 'grown up' in our thinking. However, in this day and age, we still poke fun at what we do not understand. It is my belief those who may declare Unity's Philosophy is foolishness come from a background which believes that God has a split persona, one of benevolence and the other punitive.

How many times have you heard people 'accuse' God by saying He punishes people for their misdeeds and therefore, are secretly afraid they too will be punished? There are those who have claimed, "He may or may not answer prayers." This mindset creates a chain reaction of negative thinking about God, themselves, and the world. These negative attitudes are the reason so many 'good' people suffer. Blame thrust onto God instead of taking responsibility for, and recognizing the power of one's own thoughts and attitudes.

In the Bible, the Hebrew and Greek words, which translated mean salvation and health, are often interchangeable. Jesus emphasized right thinking. Right thinking is the greatest form of salvation. Right thinking is the greatest form of health. Within you is a Power, and this Power is biased on the side of health. It does everything it can to keep you whole. Twenty-four hours a day, it supervises the complicated operation of your body. If you stop to think about it, there have been countless occasions when this Power has proven itself in your life, and in the life of someone you know.

Someone may be critically ill, not expected to live, and suddenly with no explanation, the tide is turned and the patient survives. Why? The doctors do not seem to have an answer. Oh. there are some who may say 'it was his/her strong will to live' Strong Will, yes, because Will is also a Power, and with that Power deep within you is the seed of perfection, the wholeness that is released when we know and call it forth by deliberate, persistent, right-thinking.

In the past, we have been asleep to the fact that within us lay all the Power needed for an abundant life. We have not understood, as God's offspring, we inherited His Power. We may have heard we are His children all our lives, but not fully understood the true meaning of our relationship.

The disciple who represents this faculty is Philip. His name means, lover of horses-horses represent power. This ability establishes Spiritual dominion in thought and feeling, and it assures the success of starting and completing things.

The voice is the instrument used to execute this Power. When in love the voice is soft and gentle; when feeling energetic the voice becomes strong and exhilarated; when angry loud and disturbing; when ill low and mournful. The words we use enhance these emotions.

I used to think the mind was contained in the brain, but know now that it is contained in every cell of the body. In Charles Fillmore's book, *Atom Smashing Power of the Mind,* he explains the influence of thought on the body. He said that 'like-minded thoughts,' rooted in consciousness, group together to repair the body. If this is hard to imagine think of your mind as fertile soil and the thoughts therein as seeds. As you hold on to similar thoughts, they begin to grow and spread. Charles was able to state this emphatically, because not only was he a witness to his wife's healing, but he had first hand knowledge through his own. He proved and knew through the renewal of the mind <u>all things are possible</u>..."*And be not conformed to this world: but be ye transformed by the renewing of your mind, that ye may prove what is that good, and acceptable, and perfect, will of God.*" (Romans 12:2) Charles also knew God's Will for His children was/is wholeness.

It is difficult for us to believe that the mind has so much power because we see the body as a solid mass of flesh and bone. We tend to believe in what our senses report to us; we believe in what we can see and touch. Anything not seen, 'invisible,' does not insure confidence, especially something as intangible as 'a Power of the mind.'

There is nothing solid about the body, it is 80% water; the skeleton is filled with a fluid substance making the bone soft, pliable and porous. Therefore, since the body is mostly fluid, it is conceivable that thoughts, which are mental vibrations or impulses, can move easily in and through it to build it up or tear it down. It all depends on one's thought system.

> *"Have faith in God. For verily I say unto you, that whosoever shall say unto this mountain, Be thou removed,...and shall not doubt in his heart, but shall believe that... which he saith shall come to pass; he shall have whatsoever he saith." (Mark 11:22, 23)*

The power of healing was erased from the consciousness of man, hundreds of years ago. For three hundred years, after Jesus walked the earth, there were a great many healings performed. As the church became more prosperous, the thought that the power to heal was a sign of 'High Spiritual Power' began to grow. However, there were people performing healings who were not high in the church. This caused jealousy, and so healing by the 'common' folk was forbidden. As Spiritual healing subsided, healing through medicine became popular with the masses. You see, it became a lot easier to rely on another human being; therefore, steadfast faith diminished.

In 529 A.D., the emperor Justinian, to show his disapproval of the use of medicine above faith, closed the medical schools of Athens. In 1215, to add his support in the disapproval of medical healing, Pope Innocent the Third condemned surgery, and all who practiced medicine. Then in 1428, the dissection of the body was pronounced sacrilegious, and the study of anatomy condemned. Therefore, it is no wonder that Faith healing being denounced confused the people. It was not clear to them where the church stood on healing.

Plato told the Greek physicians the reason they were unable to heal was their ignorance of the nature of the soul.

Unity teaches that man is a three-fold being, Spirit, Soul and Body. Spirit is our Oneness with God; Soul, our consciousness, which includes the conscious and subconscious minds. The body is the out picturing of the soul. In other words, <u>the body shows forth "thoughts held in mind."</u> Psychologists have admitted that most disease is self-inflicted punishment, and comes from a sense of guilt. When the mind cannot release guilt, it shows forth in the body as illness. You may or may not believe this, but isn't it worth your time and effort to change your thought patterns on the off-chance that it could be true?

Today more and more people are returning to first century Christianity that promised healing to all who had faith and <u>believed</u> in God's Law of wholeness. There is nothing new about the Power of the mind over the body. The ancient Babylonians were experts in their uses of psychosomatic, mental techniques, and hypnotism. The Hebrews looked upon disease as a result of committing a 'sin,' (which really means making a mistake; we make the mistake of turning our backs on God when we think He is not protecting us; therefore that 'mistake' is a sin) and they did not feel that they had to accept, or tolerate, disease.

When Moses' sister, Miriam, criticized him for marrying into another race, she contracted leprosy. Moses healed her by prayer. Criticism of one's self and others is a major factor in one's health. Physicians accredit Hippocrates with being the Father of medicine, but the ancients believed that Hermes was the Father of healing. His teaching contained some of the great truths that are rediscovered today. He taught that the one primary cause of ill health was unhealthy mental attitudes, such as depression, hate, resentment, criticism, jealousy, and possessiveness. He further taught that such thinking resulted in ulcers, tumors, fevers, tuberculosis, paralysis and all types of nervous conditions. The ancient also believed that germs were a creation of man's evil thoughts; they were the <u>result</u>, not the cause.

Our co-founder agreed with this and said-the physicians take for granted germs exist as an integral part of the natural world. Metaphysicians say that germs are manifested as a result of anger, revenge, fear, and impure thinking. These germs, created and named by man, have enough intelligence to come forth when called. A change of mind will change the character of the germ. Love, courage, peace, strength, and good will form the character and build healthy bodies. The dynamic energy we can release through the right use of conscious thought is unfathomable. Since our thoughts change our bodies, our deliberate thoughts will change a diseased body to a healthy one.

Jesus said, *"…whatsoever thou shalt bind on earth shall be bound in heaven: and whatsoever thou shalt loose on earth shall be loosed in heaven."* (Matthew 16:19) This states quite plainly <u>mind</u> is the <u>maker,</u> <u>thoughts</u> have <u>power</u>, as <u>within</u> so <u>without</u>. You are divine and have the potential for perfection; the tool is thought, use the tool and discover what you can demonstrate in your life. <u>You</u> have the Power! Physician, heal thyself!

God is blessing you now!

CHAPTER XVI:
UNDERSTANDING

Good Morning!

"Happy is the man that findeth wisdom, and the man that getteth understanding. For the merchandise of it is better than the merchandise of silver, and the gain thereof than fine gold. She is more precious than rubies: and all the things thou canst desire are not to be compared unto her. Length of days is in her right hand; and in her left hand riches and honor. Her ways are ways of pleasantness, and all her paths are peace. She is a tree of life to them that lay hold upon her: and happy is everyone that retaineth her. The Lord by wisdom hath founded the earth; by understanding hath he established the heavens." (Proverbs 3:13-19)

This morning's message will deal with Spiritual Understanding. This is another of God's gifts, one more Power that is part of our inheritance. I do not speak of the understanding that comes from knowledge; I speak of the understanding, which comes from within, from the heart.

I feel it is important, in the beginning of this talk, to emphasize the fact that whenever we speak of any one Power, we keep in mind that closely associated with each of them is Faith. In order to recognize and comprehend, we must believe. *"But wilt thou know, O vain man, that faith without works is dead?"* (James 2:20)

A Unity minister came up with an idea to help increase one's faith; he called it "Tabbing." When there is something you need to increase your belief in, you 'tab' it by repeating to yourself, "I totally accept and believe ___ ___." After conditioning the mind for days, weeks, or months if necessary, the belief strengthens and becomes faith. One comes to the realization not I believe, but I know!

We form our beliefs through parental guidance, friends, and school. However, when we <u>know</u> something, we know it with our very being; this knowing comes from Spiritual Understanding.

In the above scripture, Solomon enlightens us when he says a wise man is happy, but a man who has understanding has it all. What is this understanding that we call Spiritual? First, it is a Divine Idea in the mind of God. As an idea, it is absolute intelligence itself, pure knowingness. Within man it is one of the twelve Powers, the leader of this Power is the disciple Thomas. When we activate this Power, we are able to perceive the Truth, which is within, under, and through all appearances. We 'see' clearly without judgment or criticism. Spiritual Understanding is the revelation of Truth from within our own consciousness. It is our intuition that still small voice within. This Power can be cultivated in the same manner as the rest through prayer, meditation, and study.

When Jesus asked Peter who he thought He was, Peter replied, "*Thou art the Christ.*" Jesus then said, "*Blessed art thou...for flesh and blood hath not revealed it unto thee, but my Father which is in heaven.*" (Matthew 16:16, 17) Jesus was referring to Peter's use of Spiritual Understanding; he listened to the still small voice within.

I would like to make clear that there is a difference between Spiritual Understanding and intellectual knowledge. Intellectual knowledge comes first. We gather facts from books, teachers, etc; this is surface knowledge taken in consciousness and filed away. Anyone with enough facts in one's head is knowledgeable; however, it takes real wisdom to discern the meaning of the inner Truth contained within the facts. Here are the facts:

<u>You are the offspring of God.</u>

<u>You are made the very image and likeness of God</u>

God is whole and perfect; therefore, <u>you are whole and perfect.</u>

God cannot be hurt, sick, or afraid. <u>You cannot be hurt, sick, or afraid by Divine right.</u>

This is your inheritance; <u>this is the Truth of you!</u>

Intellectually, we read these words and they are just that, nice words maybe, but words nonetheless. However, if you can absorb them and feel a stirring within then you are listening with Spiritual Understanding. You are on the way to manifesting the abundance promised by Jesus the Christ. If this seems difficult to comprehend, then I ask only that you indulge me and listen, with an open heart, to the prompting within.

Jesus' purpose, His mission in life, was to teach to the masses the divinity within them, and to awaken in the individual consciousness, the understanding of his own Oneness with the Father. The same Oneness that Jesus discovered to be true. He began teaching by emphasizing love is the key. Do unto others, turn the other cheek, love your enemies; working with these principles is taking the necessary steps to 'renewing the mind'; then He instructed the masses to seek 'within' the Kingdom of Heaven. Never did he suggest the Kingdom was a place far off, just the opposite. He said, *"Neither shall they say, Lo here! or lo there! for, behold, the Kingdom of God is within you."* (Luke 17:21) He also promised, once found God would reveal Himself. Can you imagine how wonderful life could be? To seek God and find Him within, and once found, the freedom of allowing Him to show us the way to have more love, life, and power over every type of illness, and/or sorrow. It would be the elimination of fear!

I cannot reveal this Truth in all its glory to you. I can only repeat words already spoken, and experiences encountered. You must find and know God for yourself. He lives within you, He speaks to you; <u>you alone</u> must discover His Presence and hear His still small voice. I can tell you how, but you must do the work. Through prayer and meditation, we achieve direct communication with God.

The first step in gaining Spiritual Understanding is the desire for it, the second to realize that you were born with this ability, and the third working to bring it forth. Understanding is one of the twelve faculties that serve the Christ nature.

<u>T</u>otally <u>a</u>ccept the <u>b</u>elief that within you is an understanding that is Spiritual in origin and purpose. Listen for the intuitive or still small voice, and accept the truth that it will speak to you. Turn from the clamor of the outer voices and concentrate on the inner. Know your Oneness with God;

know He wishes to manifest more of Himself through you. Learn to love instead of hate; forgive instead of holding a grudge.

You may ask why someone should take the time and effort to develop Spiritual Understanding especially if there may be a doubt it even exists. Honestly, you have nothing to lose and everything to gain; you will achieve clearer insight, a peace of mind, an inner calm, and a sense of knowing who you are.

Everyone is searching; everyone wants peace, and yearns to have more good in their lives, which in reality means more God. God created a living world. Living means growing and changing. This is accomplished first within and then without.

Earlier, I spoke of Faith going hand in hand with the other twelve powers. First, we believe, then we have faith, and then we create. That is Faith <u>with</u> works. Jesus spoke many times, about what the 'Power of Faith' will do for us; He also spoke of those who 'professed' to have faith in the twenty-third chapter of Matthew (v.2, 3)

> *"Then spake Jesus to the multitude, and to his disciples, Saying, The scribes and the Pharisees sit in Moses seat: All therefore whatsoever they bid you observe, that observe and do; but do not ye after their works: for they say and do not."*

Jesus goes on to say how the Pharisees put burdens on the people. How they act so pompous citing scripture, putting on a front, and enjoying the seat at the head of the feasts and synagogue, Most of all, they liked being called Rabbi; this was a very high honor in the day.

It does not take a Bible scholar to interpret these words. Simply put, beware of hypocrites! We cram our intellect with Truth, but do not live it. We look to God, but do not 'let' Him. There are those who believe they are spiritual, simply because they know Bible verse. As the Pharisees, there are those who know only in their heads and so proclaim, "I believe this, so you must believe." This is not Truth for Truth is freedom, the freedom to believe and do as guided from within.

I stand before you this morning telling you this is what I believe, but I will not tell you that you must believe it also; your beliefs must come from <u>your</u> own heart.

Unity teaches we are Spiritual Beings. I believe within each of us is the Kingdom of God which contains the knowledge and answers to all problems. We cannot find God, or the Kingdom through man; we find it in and through Spirit. By means of study, being still, and most of all by believing, you will receive. *"Be still, and know…"* (Psalm 46:10) God is always pouring more of Himself into our lives.

On one of my visits to Unity Village, I heard the story of a woman who left a pair of scissors on her car and could not find them. In some 'unknown' way, she received two pair of scissors. She saw this as a demonstration of good. Now, you may think this a silly example; however, the woman saw it as God working in her life. The moral here-if you take all things that come to you, big and small, and see it as Spirit working in your life, it will open the door to greater demonstrations. When you have faith in the Spiritual side of <u>every</u> experience then every experience will manifest more good.

Those who have faith in themselves are successful in life. Those who have faith in their doctors' are healed; those who have faith in their fellow man are loved and respected because God is in the midst of all experiences bringing about the solution.

Jesus taught the early Christians to have faith in God; they did, and as a result, miraculous things occurred. However, as time evolved man became more enamored with worldly things. Christians, in later years, separated from 'the idea of the Spirit within' and faith 'appeared' to lose its energy; rumors circulated that miracles had occurred solely to prove Jesus as the Son of God. New Thought, founded on the teachings <u>of</u> Jesus, is <u>not</u> 'new'. It has reestablished the Truth that Faith in God, steadfast faith in what you believe, and the use of prayer <u>will</u> move mountains. Did not Jesus say, *"Verily, verily, I say unto you, He that believeth on me, the works that I do shall he do also; and greater works than these shall he do also…"* (John 14:12) Spiritual Understanding fortifies faith in whatever you do. Have faith in your own power, capacity, and ability, and you will accomplish 'greater works!'

In all our experiences, we should condemn nothing, but be alert in knowing God is in the midst of all situations. If you feel challenged, do not claim there is an angry God out there-somewhere, punishing you. Understand whatever you are <u>growing</u> through is the result of your own thoughts and actions. Pronounce nothing 'evil.' Change your mind and change the condition.

Peter tried to walk on water and as soon as he looked down-he doubted, he began to sink. Whenever we see the negative side of life, it weakens us. If we have Faith, we do not look to appearance; if we have Spiritual Understanding, we realize Faith will work because Spirit will guide and bring us safely to shore.

Seek God in the midst of you. "*Trust in the Lord with all thine heart; and lean not unto your own understanding. In all thy ways acknowledge him, and he shall direct thy paths.*" (Proverbs 3:5) Allow Him to lead you to heights yet undreamed of.

God bless you!

CHAPTER XVII:
W<small>ILL</small>

Good Morning!

Jesus said to the woman of Samaria, "*If thou knewest the gift of God, and who it is that saith to thee, Give me to drink; thou wouldest have asked of him, and he would have given thee living water.*" (John 4:10) I say to you this morning, "if you knew the will of God for you, you would say, yes, yes, yes!'

"*In the beginning was the Word, and the Word was with God, and the Word was God.*" (John 1:1) In the beginning, there was energy, God. This energy reflected on itself. It was perfect, whole, and in it contained all Power to become and do; filled with Divine Creative Ideas. One idea became a thought, and the thought became word, "*And the Word was made flesh, and dwelt among us, and we beheld his glory, the glory as of the only begotten of the Father, full of grace and truth.*" (John 1:14) That Word, that perfect idea, was/is 'the Christ.' My goal this morning is to reinforce the Truth, as we know it, that <u>God is individualized in man, in you, as the Christ.</u>

God lives, moves, has His being in man, just as man lives, moves, and has his being in God. Let us imagine that as parents, we could separate a part of ourselves and perch on our children's shoulder; we would go everywhere with them, be there to guide and direct them. We could say, 'watch out, that will harm you, or O.K., that is good;' if this were possible, would we not guide and direct them to their highest good? Is not our Father/our Creator so much greater than we are? Jesus described God as a Spirit- He has no gender, and so I lovingly say, <u>He is</u> on our shoulder, <u>She</u> is in our hearts, <u>It</u> is whispering in our ears to do, and be, the highest and best we can be as God's Expression here on earth. In order to describe God, Jesus called him Father to give us a personal relationship with Him, and to communicate to us that God wants only that we experience His goodness. That, dear ones, is His Will!

The disciple, who represents Will, is Matthew, and he goes hand in hand with Thomas, Spiritual Understanding. If man does not use his Will with Spiritual Understanding, creatively, in a Divine way, for the highest and best for all, it becomes destructive.

For too long, man has believed that God's Will can mean suffering, and that we should be pleased that God has shown favor by inflicting pain. Balderdash! I certainly would not inflict pain on any of my children; just the opposite, when they hurt, I hurt, and I want to ease their pain.

"*...God is love.*" (1 John 4:8) Jeremiah 'heard' God, "*saying, I have loved thee with an everlasting love: therefore with loving kindness have I drawn thee.*" (Jeremiah 31:3) God being Love, showering His Love upon us, how then can we give credence to anything other than God desiring good for us?

Unity teaches God's Will for us is <u>our own hearts desire</u>. This is an idea, which takes deep thought and contemplation. You see, we are so full of erroneous teachings that we balk at anything, which seems to bring us good. How many times have you said, "This is too good to be true." How many of you would be suspicious if you were walking down the street and someone was handing out one hundred dollar bills? Immediately, you would think, "What does he want? "There must be a catch." "Why is he giving this to me?" The suspicion comes from a feeling of mistrust and unworthiness; not being worthy stems from the belief in being a 'sinner.' It is my belief that before we take our first breath, buried deep in the recesses of our subconscious, there is the idea of 'sin,' but also the desire to be 'worthy' of God. This causes conflict and struggle. In Truth, we are here to learn how to overcome this design. It may take many incarnations, and great diligence, to "*...be ye transformed by the renewing of your mind...*" (Romans 12:2) and to grow in consciousness from the thought, "*...I am a worm...*" (Psalms 22:6), to "*...Ye are Gods; and all of you are children of the Most High.*" (Psalms 82:6.) Jesus verified this when he said in John 10:34, "*Is it not written in your law, I said, Ye are gods?*"

When I first was introduced to New Thought, one of the many books I read was *Power Through Constructive Thinking* by Emmet Fox. In it, he says our purpose in life, or God's Will for us, is our hearts desire. I told a friend of mine that did not make sense. She asked me what I would I like to do, and if the opportunity was given me to have one wish granted what would I chose. I replied that I had always wanted to be a singer, but never thought I was good enough. She then asked what kind of songs and without hesitation, and much to my surprise, I said, "Hymns." I thought about this for a time and decided that maybe I was supposed to join or form a gospel group. I bought music, and approached people about my idea, but it just would not jell. I was very confused. Some time later, I walked into a Unity church and knew my purpose; God's Will for me was to spread the word, not in song, but in speech.

Now here is a perfect example of how the subconscious mind rules us. When I went out to Unity Village to be interviewed for ministerial school, one of the interviewing ministers asked me, "How do you know what you want is God's Will and not your own willfulness?" I sat there silent-within me, I was screaming, "God's Will is my will," but at the same time I was afraid to answer because, who was I to think I was good enough to speak for God? I knew the Truth of my being intellectually but did not feel 'worthy' to express it.

The Will of God is absolute good for mankind, and all creation; this is not said enough. The trees and flowers allow God's Will to come forth as they grow without hindrance because they adapt themselves to their conditions. There is a unique plan for all creation. The plan for the rose is to express its perfection in beauty and fragrance. A bird expresses itself as it soars in the air and its song enhances its beauty. We too have a unique pattern-the Christ Spirit within; purpose, promise, pleasure, love, and law are all contained in God's Will for us. Let me illustrate...

<u>His Purpose</u>:	"*Ye are gods; and all of you are children of the most High.*" (Psalms 82:6)
<u>His Promise</u>:	"*Be ye therefore perfect, even as your Father which is in heaven is perfect.*" (Matthew 5:48)
<u>His Pleasure</u>:	"*... it is your Father's good pleasure to give you the kingdom.*" (Luke 12:32)
<u>His Love</u>:	"*...This is my beloved Son, in whom I am well pleased.*" (Matthew 3:17)
<u>His Law</u>:	"*...I will put the law in their inward parts, and in their hearts; I will write it, and will be their God, and they shall be my people.*" (Jeremiah 31:33)

This is what God wants us to <u>know and accept!</u>

When I discovered Unity things began to happen in my life to fortify the teachings. I wanted to shout from the housetops, "Come and see what I have found. Let me share my joy with you." However, I soon discovered what the scripture meant, *"Give not that which is holy unto the dogs, neither cast ye your pearls before swine…"* (Matthew 7:6) I do not quote this to call names; I use this only as an example. I soon discovered others did not see what I perceived as wondrous, and so in the beginning of my searching, I learned to be quiet about my joy.

There is the three-fold nature of God, which is Father, Son, and Holy Ghost/Spirit, but there is also the three-fold nature of man:Spirit, Soul, and body. Spirit is the wholeness of God within; Soul is our consciousness which is made up of the conscious and subconscious minds; the body is the expression or out picturing of the soul. We have free will to think and do, as we believe. Our thoughts are in the recesses of our mind (Soul). Therefore, belief in wholeness will produce a healthy body just as belief in illness will manifest disease, *"For as he thinketh in his heart, so is he…" (P*roverbs 23:7)

If we do not understand God's Will-His idea for us, we may live our lives without any definite direction or purpose. There will be those who do not see the importance of this and even scoff but turning to God in prayer, for direction, will not only keep you healthy in mind and body, but successful in life as well.

Can you not see that God's Will can only mean abundant good? Think about it. Since God lives within, and expresses without, by allowing Him to show the way you draw to you only the highest good. Anyone can experience God if he/she releases the selfish attitude that comes from the willfulness of the 'me/mine' frame of mind. How often we have heard the words, "Let go and let God" but how often do we do it? We equate letting go to the way we let go a deep breath. As we exhale, it feels as if a part of us is released. That is how one feels when we let go of troublesome situations, circumstances and people. Would it not better to release than hold on to negative situations, and continue to feel up tight, nervous, and frightened? Once 'letting go' is mastered, *"…the crooked shall be made straight, and the rough ways shall be made smooth;"* (Luke 3:5)

I said earlier, the two Powers that go hand in hand are Will and Spiritual Understanding. When we use our will without realizing the Truth about our identity, (Spiritual beings) and use 'human' understanding (which usually comes from a me/mine attitude) then Will becomes willfulness. Mistakes are the result of willful behavior. This behavior is selfish, emotional, and creates tension. Releasing and declaring, "*Thy Will be done*" brings a calmness. It is in surrendering that we find peace.

Jesus taught us God's Will "...*I am come that they might have life, and that they might have it more abundantly.*" (John 10:10) I, the Christ, the Spirit of God <u>in</u> man, I have come forth to tell you, God wants only the best for you; God wants you to live life to the fullest.

By healing the sick and raising the dead, Jesus proved God wants us to be healthy. He told parables about sowing seeds to help us understand 'mind is the maker.' When we sow seeds of faith, love, strength, and power, God's Divine ideas can come forth through us! He fed the masses to prove God is our Source of supply. He told parables such as the Ten Talents (found in Luke 19:12) to explain God multiplies our good when we open ourselves to giving and sharing.

If anyone believes that God inflicts pain and punishment, creates disasters, takes loved ones from us, then they are worshipping a God of duality and <u>not</u> the God Jesus taught and loved. Believing in duality separates us from the consciousness of His love, and blocks His power to work in our lives.

Spiritual Healing depends on faith. We cannot have faith and limit God at the same time. If we cannot act without a sign, if we cannot give without an increase-first, if we cannot believe in health <u>before</u> the healing, then we cannot trust God or His Will; nor can we know the power of His love. A positive attitude blesses!

Pray, talk to God, and whenever possible, think of God's love for you. It is this understanding that will help you to realize that God's Will is only for your good. Meditate, listen for His answers, release, surrender, let go, and submit your willfulness to His Will; proclaim without hesitation, "Let <u>our</u> will be done on earth as it is in heaven."

God blesses you now!

CHAPTER XVIII:
Divine Order

Good Morning!

There is a simple prayer in Unity. When we find ourselves in unpleasant situations, or in need of a quick solution, we say five words, "Father, I declare Divine Order." It may sound too simple, but it does work whether you are in, or observing, a heated confrontation, or something as undemanding and simple as a parking place. My grandchildren love it when we go somewhere and a parking place seems to open up miraculously. They do not know I declare Divine Order as soon as I pull out of my garage. Order is the first Law of the Universe. The planets, sun, moon, stars, trees, and flowers all attest to that. It makes sense the Universe would not exist without order. We know God created the Universe, and another name for God is Law, ergo Order is Law.

> Charles Fillmore defined science: "Science is the systematic and orderly arrangement of knowledge. Spiritual science, which is the orderly arrangement of the truths of Being, does not always conform to intellectual standards, but it is still scientific. Spiritual science treats of absolute ideas, while mental science treats of limited thoughts."
>
> (Taken from <u>The Revealing Word</u> by Charles Fillmore)

The disciple who represents Order is James the Less, son of Alphaues. This faculty, when called forth, gives one the ability to progress harmoniously, to evolve in a creative way, and gives one the ability to see things in proper progression.

When Charles and Myrtle Fillmore attended New Thought classes given by Mary Baker Eddy, the founder of Christian Science, their studies were primarily scientific. This did not have the appeal to Myrtle as it did to Charles, because she <u>had</u> experienced God. She had felt His Presence. I feel as Myrtle did and I believe, in order to understand God and the Universe, there is a need to delve deeper not only emotionally, but scientifically as well.

Jesus said, "*God is a Spirit: and they that worship him must worship him in spirit and in truth.*" (John 4:24) The science of Spirit is the only real science because Spirit never changes. To fully understand and know God, law, order, we need to awaken to the possibilities, which lie within us. Those who have studied *Lessons in Truth* by Emily Cady know she imparts to the reader a request - they need not understand, or agree, with what she has written. All that is necessary is an open mind and a willingness to learn. Therefore, to embark on this quest all one need do is allow the Holy Spirit to guide them. "*But there is a spirit in man: and the inspiration of the Almighty giveth them understanding.*" (Job 32:8) We begin by recognizing what God is and what our relationship is to Him.

God is the origin of all things. We are the offspring of this Mighty Power; therefore, we have the same characteristics as our creator. The knowledge that God is the Father-Mother of all of us opens the way for us to understand not only our relationship to Him, but our creative nature as well. The creation story tells us that God created by word, "A*nd God said, Let there be…*" (Genesis 1:3) We, as His offspring are blessed with the same power of creation, 'the word!'

We have been in confusion because of a belief in two powers, good and evil. As a result, we have become skeptical; we cry, "Don't tell me God is all good when he lets bad things happen." Listen closely God does <u>not</u> do anything. He has <u>finished</u> His work. "*And on the seventh day God ended his work which he had made; and he rested on the seventh day from all his work which he had made.*" (Genesis 2:2) He has passed the gauntlet on to us to continue doing His work. He is Ever Present to help and guide, to work through us, <u>when we ask;</u> otherwise, we are on our own. Y'know, when things are running smoothly it is easy for us to see the relationship of cause and effect, take the credit for doing well; however, hit a bump in the road and no way do we see our mistakes. If appearances are out of harmony, God is not to blame; truthfully what has happened is a <u>misapplication</u> of the law.

The realization and understanding that we have inherited the Power to create by speaking the word is the first step in awakening. <u>Words are thoughts manifested</u>! In order to know this, we need to comprehend that we are one with Our Creator. God is Spirit. We are made in His image; <u>we</u> are Spirit. Spirit cannot be hurt, sick, or afraid. Spirit cannot be hurt by anyone or anything; it cannot be sick for sickness is an illusion; it cannot be afraid because fear is an appearance; <u>fear is not a Power</u>. Here is an acronym for you to memorize and take into consciousness, <u>F</u>alse <u>E</u>vidence <u>A</u>ppearing <u>R</u>eal!

God is the <u>only</u> Power! We are one with God! When we allow this Truth to infiltrate every fiber of our being, it brings with it a freedom and a knowing-how to correct and improve any challenge.

We speak of the conscious and subconscious mind; there is a super conscious mind as well. *"Let this mind be in you, which was also in Christ Jesus: Who, being in the form of God, thought it not robbery to be equal with God:"* (Philippians 2:5,6). When we trust it, we become open to the voice of God and deep things are revealed to us.

God, Universal Mind, Primal Cause, Father, Mother, Higher Power, All Good, it does not matter what you call it. The Hindus called it Brahma. They believed that Brahma is a being of such magnitude that man shrinks into nothingness in its presence. Whether its name is Brahma, Universal Mind, Father, or God, that Presence-in its entirety-is within every one of us-His creations.

Jesus lovingly taught that God is within, not at a distance, and definitely not in some far away place called Heaven. Spirit is the seat of Power and its home is within man. Paul made the revelation: *"One God and Father of all, who is above all, and through all, and in you all."* (Ephesians 4:6) Does it not make sense that the Power, which sustains the universe, also sustains His children?

The desire to understand God has caused a great deal of seeking; some succeed, some flounder, possibly, because of the many points of view and the different interpretations theologians and scholars have given to God and to the scriptures. Mind is the key. When we truly discern the science-the orderly way the mind functions-we will solve the mysteries of creation. The definition of mind and spirit are almost identical in the dictionary. Considering this, if mind and spirit are synonymous then there is no great mystery about Spiritual things: *"Know ye not that ye are the temple of God, and that the Spirit of God dwelleth in you?"* (1 Corinthians 3:16) God is within us as our minds are in our bodies. God creates through the Power of mind; thought is the vehicle used. It is through our thoughts that we find God!

Divine ideas are those, which come from God. They are Love, Life, Substance, and Intelligence; they reside in the mental realm where there is an inexhaustible supply. We receive ideas from God. Let me point out, God is the giver of ideas, but man has free will and choice; therefore he may misuse them. That is the only reason lack can appear.

Charles Fillmore taught Practical Christianity. He said it was the combination of the right relationship of ideas, and the knowledge of right thought. As a student of Truth, all studies and activities begin with the understanding of oneness; there is One Presence, One Power in the Universe. God is Omnipresent. God is Universal Mind working in and through all things. If anyone is skeptical about the existence of God, or ambivalent about his or her beliefs, he/she will receive their answer though prayer, persistent prayer. However, one needs to be willing to seek God because He does not force Himself on anyone.

Many will ask, "If we are offspring of Divine Mind, then why are we not conscious of its Presence?" Well, folks, it is our own fault. God gave us a beautiful gift - the Power to bring into visibility that which is not seen. We took that Power and formed a realm that separated us, in consciousness, from Him. We made God in our image and placed Him way beyond reach, high on a throne. Jesus, however, taught in the parable of the Prodigal Son, that when we grow weary of limitation and strife, we only have to head for home and our Creator will rush out to meet us with open arms.

Jesus knew, *"I and my Father are one."* (John 10:30); He knew and taught we are all one in God. *"At that day ye shall know that I am in my Father, and ye in me, and I in you."* (John 14:20) Jesus constantly referred to His consul, and spent whole nights in meditation and prayer to know their oneness. We too can have an 'awakening' and come into the understanding of the Truth of our being through meditation.

The practice of daily meditation, fifteen to twenty minutes a day, is the beginning of opening the mind to the conscious awareness of God. Honestly, I know how to tell you how to meditate, but you must experience it for yourself; then no one can take away that which you know from within you. Experiencing the Presence of Divine Mind can not be explained in words. It is referred to in parables and can be likened unto this or that, but it can never be described.

We have the ability to receive the ideas of Divine Mind in consciousness. No two individuals are alike because, although we each draw our ideas from Divine Mind, the fulfillments of those ideas come from our own individual understanding, realization, and faith.

So what is the Science of Being? We teach that God is Principle, Law, Being, Mind, Spirit, All-good, Omnipotent, Omniscient, Omnipresent, Unchangeable, Creator, First Cause, Father-Mother, and Source of all that is. We, being the <u>very image and likeness of God</u>, are Spiritual Beings, living in a Spiritual World, governed by Spiritual Law. We created in His image-Spirit; therefore, we are God in manifestation. We are one with God-not the wholeness of-but a part of God. We receive guidance and direction in mind as ideas; and ideas have expression, and all that we manifest in our individual worlds are the result of the ideas we hold in mind.

The universe maintains an orderly manner; the mind works in an orderly manner-although it may not appear to do so at times, the body responds to the direction of the mind, in an orderly manner. All things are in divine order.

Paul revealed in scripture the greatest gift God has given us: "...*But we have the mind of Christ.*" (1 Corinthians 2:16) Hold fast to the idea of unconditional love, health, and the abundance of God's supply. Prove to yourself that you are one with your brother, Jesus, one with your Father, God, and one with all humankind.

God Blesses you and so do I.

CHAPTER XIX:
The Importance of Zeal

Good Morning!

It has been reported, in his 94th year of life, Charles Fillmore sprang from his bed and wrote, "I fairly sizzle with life and enthusiasm and spring forth to do the things that ought to be done by me." Isn't that fantastic? I venture to guess that there are those of us here this morning, one-half that age, who find it difficult to spring out of bed, much less have the enthusiasm to greet the day. The problem being, we do not seem to become fired up over things. We have misplaced that air of expectancy and today, I would like to help you recapture it.

Paul was a good example of zeal/enthusiasm. Before his Damascus event, he was known as Saul and was a deeply religious Pharisee. Educated as a Rabbi, he believed in the perfect compliance of the law, and therefore, believed in the persecution of those who were against his God. He fired up his determination by condemning his enemies with one breath, then praising God with the next.

However, on the way to Damascus, to carry out his persecution of the 'lawless,' there was a great light that shone upon him; it was so bright it blinded him. He heard the voice of Jesus the Christ saying, *"Saul, Saul why persecutest thou me?"* (Acts 9:4) Understandably, Saul frightened, and in awe, he asked what was wanted of him. He was instructed to go to the city and there he would be told what to do. The men with him, although they heard the voice but saw no one, helped the now blind man to his feet and continued on their journey. Once there Saul regained his sight. (Acts 9:1-20) This experience enriched, illumined, and enlightened Saul, who was known from then on as Paul. It was the beginning of a new way of life; one filled with teaching and preaching the gospel of Jesus the Christ.

Allow me to digress for a moment in order to point out that this experience proves that no matter how far we stray from God, we can always return, or awaken, to the Truth within us. Saul had not only lost his way but he had <u>absolutely no belief</u> in what the followers of Jesus taught. In spite of that, Jesus chose him to be His representative. There may be times when we despair, give up believing in anything, but Truth remains. God waits patiently for us to remember, to see a small spark of escape from hopelessness, and when we ask, "What do you want me to do?" He will send a league of angels to help release us from our burdens. *"Come unto me, all ye that labour and are heavy laden, and I will give you rest."* (Matthew 11:28)

Paul had an enormous amount of zeal and enthusiasm; first as the champion of the law and the prophets, and then, when his sight returned he became an advocate of Jesus. He saw the Truth! This knowledge "…*Christ in you, the hope of glory*" (Colossians 1:27) accelerated his zeal and gave him peace.

Zeal is a strong force, it is an urge, and it is an impulse that fires us up and sets into motion that which we desire. Emerson said, "Nothing great was ever achieved without enthusiasm." Isn't that so? Think about the important things that have happened in your life; remember the feeling of excitement and expectancy as they were coming into fruition.

How about the first apartment you rented, or the first house you bought? Consider how you felt anticipating the venture. Maybe it was the time when you bought your first automobile, and your joy when you drove it off the lot. Then there was the time when you interviewed for that special job, and you got it. Yes, you were nervous, but underneath the nervousness was a fire-kindled by Spirit that set it in motion. However, Zeal, as with all our Powers, needs help and must be tempered with love and understanding, or it too can become a destructive force.

Jesus had two disciples named Simon; one we know as Simon Peter who represents Faith, and the other Simon the Canaanite/Zealot. He is the one who represents Zeal/Enthusiasm. This Power gives us motivation to progress, to grow spiritually. It is the ability to express enthusiasm, to be fired up so to speak. The Psalmist said, *"For the zeal of thine house hath eaten me up;"* (69:9) meaning the desire for the material world can stagnate one, and make the Temple of God-your body, and the Kingdom of Heaven-your mind, impure.

This in no means discredits the Truth that we can have what we are entitled to, an abundant life. You see, we are so zealous in striving to solve the challenges and economic problems of our everyday life that we forget God is in the midst of us. We think there is no time to ask God for solutions, requests for guidance, for His help, in all our needs. Instead, we scheme and plan on our own, as a result we get deeper and deeper into trouble. The human being falls into the hands of greed, selfishness, and confusion.

There is even an excessive, and at times, misdirected zeal shown in the observance of religions. How many churches have split because of mistaken enthusiasm within their walls, the over-observing of rites, and forgetting the Principle that the church stands for. It is wonderful to be zealous but Spirit must guide it.

Energy is Zeal in motion. When we desire some special good in our lives, the Universe will comply; however, we must be motivated to pursue our desire with an excitement from within. Whether it is cooking an important dinner, writing a sermon, delivering mail, arguing a case before the bar, or weeding in a garden, feel exuberant and the job will be done. Desire comes before the culmination of every act; desire comes from God. The word desire means "of the father"; therefore, the desire of our hearts to accomplish, to achieve our potential, is already ours because the Spirit within has given it to us. We bring forth our dreams with excitement and enthusiasm.

I remember the first time I received the 'idea' to become a minister. I laugh at it. It wasn't the fact that I was not a college graduate, or the fact that I was a woman that bothered me; my first reaction was I was too old. "Go back to school at my age?" Then I thought, I would have to hit the books, study, do research, have hours of homework; I did not like school when I had to go, why in the world choose to go back. Therefore, I shelved the thought. However, it kept coming back to my mind, and I finally decided to tell my minister. She told me there was no such thing as age in Spirit and if it was something I really wanted 'school would not be a chore.' Those words had a freeing effect on me and I allowed the 'idea' to take hold. Suddenly eagerness began to spread through me along with a feeling of excitement. Zeal fueled me with enthusiasm.

The first night at the *Lessons in Truth* class, the minister requested that each answer given, with our written homework, include a scriptural reference. Mentally I shrank at what I thought to be an enormous quest. I had gone to

Sunday school when a child, memorized the books of the Bible, knew certain precepts and parables, but had no idea how or where to look for scriptural references. However, much to my surprise, I found that to be the best and most exciting part of the assignment. There were times when it took nearly an hour to find what I needed, but when I did, the joy of verification was worth it. To this day, I ask the same of my students, knowing it will help them have a better understanding of themselves, and the Bible.

I thank God I did not encourage the negative response I had initially, and 'give up' on that prodding to become a minister. I urge you to take seriously whatever comes to you, no matter how 'outrageous' it may appear at the time; commune with it, feel it, praise it, analyze it if you must, but do not repress the Spirit of Enthusiasm that will come with the idea. Let yourself be guided, and combined with wisdom, find the happiness and success, which is rightfully yours.

Zeal says 'Go forth'; Wisdom tempers it. Many years ago, I heard a story about a man who became obsessed with Truth teachings. He began to neglect his family, and finally his business; all he did was read and absorb all he could. This was Zeal <u>without</u> Wisdom, and in time, it affected his mind. Of course, this is an extreme example; however, do not allow zeal to run away with you. Flow with it, and allow it to motivate you, not dictate to you.

What desire, what good, what idea, is passing through your mind right now? Whatever it is know it is a prompting from God, and go with the flow. If it strikes you as 'bizarre.' at least think about it and let it simmer in consciousness for a while. Once you become receptive to it, give yourself permission to become enthusiastic and begin planning the outcome.

In Unity, we form prayer groups fashioned from a class called, "The Master Mind Principle". It involves two to six people getting together once a week, and following a program, which incurs seven steps. They are surrender, belief, decision, release (this includes the giving and asking of forgiveness), then the prayer request. The last step is to acknowledge gratefully 'the prayer answered.' Partners work together, and with the help of these faithful companions, prayers are answered. Incorporated in each step is Zeal/enthusiasm. There is a feeling of excitement in surrendering to God, and a peace in knowing-I no longer need to struggle for God is in charge. I have seen miracles occur within these Master Mind groups. God is the Power and the Glory, and there is a definite excitement in believing, in making a decision, and most of all in saying "Yes", to God.

This applies to all prayers. When you ask (the word in Arabic really means 'claim'-but that it another lesson) anticipate the answer will be 'yes' and with exuberance say "Thank You" <u>before</u> the fact.

The last step of the Master Mind states, "I go forth with a spirit of enthusiasm, excitement, and expectancy." That is your commitment to follow through.

Are you looking for a Damascus experience? Do you want more faith? Are there questions that need answering in your life? Then become enthusiastic in your seeking. Fill yourself with exuberance and face life with all its glory. God is good! Life is of God! Life is for living! Live it with expectancy. Begin right now to expect a miracle. Ask, believing, and you <u>shall</u> receive.

God Bless You!

CHAPTER XX:
Renunciation/Elimination

Good Morning!

The dictionary states, renunciation means a surrender of claim or interest, rejection. We know the meaning of elimination is to remove, be rid of, set aside, expel. Would you believe this was an important teaching of Jesus? Another of Jesus' disciples was Thaddaeus. He is the one who represents this Power, which gives one the strength to eliminate error thought from the mind.

In Unity, we call it 'denial'. There were certain beliefs and ideas held by our ancestors and imbedded in our subconscious, that caused conflict; the time has come 'to be born anew'. We accomplish this through the surrender and expulsion of these ancient beliefs.

George Bernard Shaw said, "Better keep yourself clean and bright. You are the window through which you must see the world." Paul said, "...*we see through a glass darkly*." (1 Corinthians 13:12) If the window we are seeing through is dark and murky, it is because doubt and fear cloud it. As a result, we live, work, sleep, talk, and we move in a world of self-doubt and fear. We pattern our self-image and the images of those around us, as well as the world in general, according to what we see. We live in a negative world of our own doing. I simply abhor it when I hear anyone quote Murphy's Law which states, "if there is anything bad that can happen, it will". That is a defeatist attitude that is frustrating and dangerous to the individual's well being.

The purpose of denial is to clean the window, to sweep away self-defeating pictures, concepts, attitudes, and opinions in mind that have become firmly fixed. We have one purpose in this world and that is to become more aware and attuned with our Creator. God is All Good, and every time we see something, and label it as bad (evil), or see sickness, poverty, limitation of any kind, we are keeping Him in the background. We are turning our backs and walking away, so to speak, from our God-given heritage.

The purpose of denial is not to deny something out of existence but to weaken its <u>so-called</u> power over us. Unfortunately, as long as there are those who do not seek, do not believe in God, or/and do believe there is a 'devil' with power, evil will <u>appear</u> to exist. However, once centered in God, we are aware of the Truth of our being, and know 'evil is an <u>illusion</u>, it has <u>no power</u>'. We receive this freeing knowledge through thinking 'anew'- which culminates in a change of attitude.

Those who interpret the Bible literally have taught we are 'to deny' ourselves material and physical pleasures. Throughout His teachings, Jesus emphasized, 'Life is consciousness, man is a Spiritual being made in the image and likeness of His Father, which is Spirit.' Ergo, we also do our creative work in mind in view of the fact that we are Spiritual beings. Misinterpreting His message, many have believed that denial referred to the enjoyments of life and have preached giving up of normal emotions, giving up worldly goods, and even have gone so far as suggesting one should give thanks for a sickly body. This is a denial of health, and goodness, which goes against God.

Jesus taught God is Wholeness, and as His image, He wants wholeness for His children. Jesus healed to emulate God. Unity stresses "be what you are; God's offspring", and as His offspring heir to all that He is and all He has. For too long our thinking has been limited. It is time to begin to use intelligent thinking, coupled with loving emotions, so the good that God wants for us can be recognized and expressed.

Jesus said to his disciples, *"If any man will come after me, let him deny himself, and take up his cross, and follow me."* (Matthew 16:24) In other words, if we believe in Him and what He promised us then we deny the ego, the human state, and do as He did.

We read and hear so much about the ego, but do we truly understand the true power and force it exerts over us daily? If we are in the presence of someone who is behaving arrogantly, and is full of his self-importance, we would comment, "what an ego!" On the other hand, seeing someone meek and quietly standing in the background, we would probably think he wasn't displaying any ego (although this is ego working in reverse asking for sympathy). It is so easy to see the workings of someone else's ego and be completely blind to our own at work. Jesus knew and that is why he instructed us to '*deny ourselves*'. It is the ego that tells us we are always right; the ego, which demands proof, and insists 'seeing is believing'; the ego which interferes, criticizes, and makes demands. Spirit certainly is not attributed to any of these. Ego supplies us with excuses and reasons why. It helps us create circumstances and conditions to validate 'human' behavior. You may find this hard to believe but it is our own ego, which keeps us separated from God.

Jesus accepted and proved the Divinity in man, the Christ within. The symbolism of His dying on the cross was only to reveal there was no death, only everlasting, ongoing life, and to prove man can conquer the appearance of evil. Jesus never recognized evil for he saw with a clarity, and vision the true meaning of life. His eye was single-minded always on good-on God. His mission was to bring this Truth to man-to enlighten all, then and now, that evil is no more than the absence of good. Look for and see good and evil disappears.

Unity teaches <u>affirmations,</u> the recognition and firming up of positive God inspired thoughts. However, before we can fully know the good in life, we must first deny the negative, and see it for what it is-false appearance. The first denial is, "There is no evil!" It is indeed a shocking statement, and you can very well give me examples of the evil you believe abounds. However, that word definitely brings to mind all things heinous, when in Truth; evil is no more than an <u>appearance of lack</u>, the lack of good. Evil did not exist for Jesus. He knew there was/is only One Presence and One Power in the universe, God, the Good Omnipotent!

I do not find it difficult to accept this denial because I am an all or nothing individual. I am not one to do things by degrees to say, "There could be a <u>possibility</u> that there is no evil, or I would like to believe there is no evil." Those thoughts are not for me. We have free will to choose our thoughts and beliefs, and this denial can help one to realize the Truth, there is only One Power; <u>there is only God the Good, Omnipotent.</u> Evil is an appearance.

Any new idea takes contemplation, and I would never suggest 'just accept', but I do ask you to think about it and then decide for yourself. Once you have made a decision then attack it as if you were going to jump into a cold pool on a hot summer day; take a deep breath and plunge in. Examine the possibilities and either make a leap of faith, or stay just where you are. Whatever the choice it is yours, and it is right for you.

So what are the rewards or consequences of these choices? Well, to stay in fear of evil and believe in its power will invite into your life continued confusion and disappointment. To think that disharmony and dis-ease exists gives them a power that will not only work in your life, but in the lives of those, you 'see'. We create a world of unhappiness and frustration wrought by fear. On the other hand, when we choose to work with the thought "There is no evil", we begin to recognize the problems that occur are <u>temporary.</u> God is in the midst of us and in the situations we encounter. God is our help in every need. All we need do is ask, and good will be revealed.

To place one's trust in God and put Him in charge is a freeing concept much like the little child who is lost and when found grips his mother's hand for dear life. Surrendering to God brings a release from fear. When we know in our heart of hearts that God is with us, what is there to fear? A feeling of peace takes over and with it joy and happiness. Can you really choose to continue to see evil when you attain so much by seeking and finding good?

As I said earlier, we use denials for cleansing of the mind, and then follow with affirmations. An affirmation is a strong declaration made to firm up one's belief in the reality of the Presence of God. Whenever we speak a denial, it is important to follow it with an affirmation. We can liken our minds to fertile soil, and in this soil, ideas take root and grow. Uprooting (denying) a negative idea/thought leaves a space; we then take the opportunity to plant a seed of good (an affirmation). Sowing the good/positive thought in the space, immediately, is necessary in order to thwart another negative thought from taking hold.

The first affirmation is "God is Life, Love, Intelligence, Substance, Omnipotence, Omniscience, and Omnipresence." God being all these things, how can there be evil? <u>There is only One Power.</u> You have the choice. You have dominion to call upon, listen to, and use, this One and Only Power.

Faith is the key to demonstration. Given a diagnosis of a terminal disease <u>if</u> one has faith in God, and believes in His Love and His desire for his/her wholeness, then the dis-ease will be no more. However, believe in the diagnosis, resign oneself to the appearance of the inevitable, and the inevitable will happen. Jesus said, *"I am the way, the truth, and the life: no man cometh unto the Father, but by me."* (John 14; 6) We become one with God as we follow the path Jesus chose, absolute faith, loving everyone, <u>not</u> for his or her personality but for the Spirit within; He lived this daily. He knew,

Oneness with God, and we too can know it if we allow ourselves to think as Jesus did.

Franklin Delano Roosevelt said, "There is nothing to fear, but fear itself." It is our fears that magnify, hold us back, and keep us in bondage.

> *"Or what man is there of you, whom if your son ask bread, will he give him a stone? Or if he ask a fish, will he give him a serpent? If ye then, being evil, know how to give good gifts unto your children, how much more shall your Father which is in heaven give good things to them that ask him?"* (Matthew 7:9-11)

Think about this. Let it seep into your subconscious. I will leave you with one more thought provoking scripture. *"And the Lord God caused a deep sleep to fall upon Adam, and he slept:"* (Genesis 2:21)

<u>Man still sleeps</u>! *"Awake thou that sleepest,"* (Ephesians 6:14) Awake to the reality that God lives <u>in</u> you, <u>as</u> you. There is nothing to fear. Evil, as with beauty, is in the eye of the beholder; renounce it; eliminate it from your mind. See all problems and challenges as temporary appearances and be at peace.

God Bless you all!

For my dear readers,

It occurred to me that in the above lesson, while explaining the cleansing and ultimate raising of one's consciousness using denials and affirmations, you might not be familiar with them. Therefore, on the possibility you may want to try them; I will set them down for your perusal.

It is safe to say, that throughout a normal day, we have little things that come up and disturb our peace. Meeting these vexations with a denial will help subdue those times of trial. For instance, if you say to yourself "This is not real, It cannot hurt or harm me," and do not fight it, do not give it any power, peace will return. Deny the person, action, or thoughts of another, to have influence over you, and know you are love made manifest.

Denials:

There is no evil.

There is no absence of life, substance, or intelligence anywhere.

Pain, sickness, poverty, old age, and death cannot master me, for they are not real.

There is nothing in all the universe for me to fear, for greater is He within me than he who is in the world.

We may not be aware of it, but every day we are continually affirming. We make positive statements as well as negative ones, and both of them create through our thoughts and spoken words. This being the case, it is important to speak and think only of what you desire-a healthy body, financial freedom, and loving relationships. Set goals for your life. It is also a good idea to write down what you desire. You may create your own affirmation or use those below. It is advisable to commit them to memory so you can silently recite them when needed. When you can do so, with faith, they will release you from any, and all distress, and present you with your desires.

Affirmations:

God is Life, Love, Intelligence, Substance, Omnipotence, Omniscience, Omnipresence.

I am a child, or manifestation of God, and every moment, His life, wisdom, power, flow through me. I am one with God and I am governed by His law.

I am Spirit, perfect, holy, harmonious. Nothing can hurt me or make me sick or afraid, for Spirit is God, and God cannot be sick, or hurt or afraid. I manifest my real self through this body now!

(This is my personal favorite)

God works with me to will and do whatsoever He wishes me to do, and God cannot fail!

CHAPTER XXI:
LIFE

Good Morning everyone.

Today we will talk about the last power in the series, Life. Early on in Unity, as I pictured my goals it was my desire to do everything in my power to eliminate the fear of death to my congregations. I believe if we overcome this overwhelming uncertainty, we would eliminate all fears of illness, separation, muggings, and currently, terrorism. You see, in reality, Life is Eternal, and no one or no-thing can take it away from us.

We are the very image and likeness of God; it is <u>through</u> us He lives, moves and has expression. Within our being is a seed, a potential called The Christ that is the Spirit of God in man. This seed, or idea, expresses energy, light, wisdom, understanding, and will communicate these blessings to each of us. However, it depends on our receptivity. When we allow God to advise, when we accept direction, when we let go of the human ego which shouts, "I can do it myself", when we recognize we are <u>Spiritual beings</u> clothed in skin, and there is no ending, (death) then the Spirit of God will flow freely and we will know-<u>There is only Life!</u>

God does not dictate how we are to live. He has given us free choice; He allows us to make our own decisions, walk our own path without interference. However, you know how fickle we can be. When things are going well, we smile and take credit; but as soon as something goes awry, we assume 'God willed it"-instead of taking responsibility.

In order to understand life, we must come to terms with what our beliefs are concerning death. The crucifixion was not meant to be a sad event, but proof of everlasting Life. Death was born out of ignorance. In the beginning there was no concept of death for being/spirit was brought forth out of the Eternal with a conscious knowing 'that which was and ever shall be'.

However, there came a time when restlessness began to occur and a desire to experiment with co-creating. The experimenters became so self-absorbed with the sensation of creating; they neglected to use their powers of wisdom and discernment and 'hid' from The Lord.

Allow me to digress a moment and explain, metaphysically, Lord is Spiritual man, our Divine self, the creative power within; it is the activity of the Spiritual I am. God told Moses His name was "*I AM THAT I AM.*" (Exodus 3:14) We, as His offspring, have His name. "I am" is our Spiritual name. We identify ourselves with whatever we attach our 'I am' to, and through the Power of the "I am" will manifest whatever we declare. When we are blinded by human condition, it can be destructive. In other words to proclaim, "I am poor, I am sick, I am afraid" will become prophetic statements. However, governed by Spirit, positive statements joined with-I am-give miraculous results. When the created 'beings' hid from their Lord, they left 'the Garden of Eden', the consciousness of peace, all good and eternal bliss.

Two aspects of death that have been destructive:

1- Death is final.

2- Death is something to fear.

Death is a thought, a belief, in the mind of the human consciousness. Jesus said, "*Follow me; and let the dead bury their dead.*" (Matthew 8:22) In other words, He is saying wake up and realize, "I am The Christ. I am here to tell you the Truth. Follow in my way of faith and love. I Am within you. I Am 'is' Life Eternal. To those who wish to hear they will understand, and to those who do not, leave them to their miseries."

The first concept to overcome is 'God ordained it'. Does it not seem a little ludicrous that God would ordain death, and at the same time, through man, sanction healing and wholeness? Why would he send Jesus to teach "abundant life"?

We hear repeatedly that ill health "is God's will," but I tell you God's will for us is whatever good we desire. (It is important to remember it means the highest good for all concerned; not for any selfish motive or wish that can cause harm) That is why it is so important to use the Powers of Wisdom and

Discernment to live a harmonious life, to think positive thoughts, to make your words loving, and to see all things as a process for the good of all.

It is written, "*Thou shalt also decree a thing, and it shall it be established unto thee: and the light shall shine upon thy ways.*" (Job 22:28) To have a healthy body, a loving relationship, an abundant income, one should decree it. Overcome the fear of the unknown by realizing death is but a trip from one plane to another with consciousness in tact; Life Is Consciousness!

What is death? The dictionary states it is a cessation of vital forces and action in the body; however, we are not our bodies; we are Spiritual beings. Joel Goldsmith, a writer of New Thought books, wrote, "We are in the world but not of it." When the fruit from the tree of knowledge was eaten it caused a belief in two powers, God and not-God.

The Bible says that men are 'dead' in their sins. I have no idea how the word 'sin' has come to have such an ominous influence because it simply means one who has made a mistake; separated himself/herself from God. Now, I do not mean to make light of this; it is a disparaging thing to segregate oneself (in thought) from one's Creator. You are probably thinking that you would never do such a thing; however, as soon as we give credence to two powers, we look <u>away</u> from the Omnipotent, Omniscient, Omnipresent God. I am positive that no matter what religion we were brought up in we all were taught that God is all Powerful. This being the Truth, then where in the world did the devil get all its power? Believing in two powers <u>deadens</u> one to his true reality. We are Spiritual beings, living in a Spiritual world, and governed by Spiritual law! The renewing of the mind comes from awakening to this Truth, and to the realization that God lives <u>in</u> you, <u>as</u> you. You are one with God!

Blood flows through the body; there are corpuscles in the blood, which act as little batteries with negative and positive poles. Within these batteries are the elements of life, which are constantly stimulating and revitalizing us. However, if we begin to talk about or begin to believe in the absence of life, through the power of our word, the batteries weaken. The energy of life begins to slow down due to negative thought.

Thoughts are things, which stay in the mind. When we think negatively, it holds those ideas in mind, which in turn manifest and out-picture in the body.

Joanne M. Dator

I absolutely believe, as Charles and Myrtle Fillmore the co-founders of Unity, that there is no need for illness and no need for anyone to show signs of aging. I realize that there are many who are not ready to accept this as truth. However, I also believe we are slowly beginning to awaken. More and more patients and doctors believe in the power of prayer and use positive thoughts to heal. As for aging, there is proof positive that we are slowly unfolding in this area as well. When I was a 'youngster', sixty was old. The mortality table was sixty-two for men and sixty-five for women. Look at the movies of yesteryear, if you remember the "Andy Hardy" or "The Little Rascals" movies; the parents appear like the grandparents of today. We are much more youth oriented, or, may I say, we are holding in consciousness youth, and as a result, many are living healthier lives, and living well into their nineties-some even surpassing their hundredth birthday.

"And the light shineth in darkness; and the darkness comprehended it not" (John 1:5) the Light-Spirit, and the darkness-man. We do not fully realize the Truth about Spirit and its Laws. Spirit is the highest realm of mind; achieving conscious unity with this Presence through the power of thought and word opens up a new world.

It is sad, but true, we live in a world wrought with fear. Just listen to the six o'clock news! As little ones, we learned to love God but also fear Him. As we grew older, the warning was "be wary of evildoers, and do not trust." Is it any wonder we fear the concept of death?

Perfect love casts out fear. Jesus said, *"Honor thy father and thy mother: and, Thou shalt love thy neighbor as thyself."* (Matthew 19:19) Is this so much to ask? The majority of the human race would honor their earthly parents, but fall short with others. Treating a loved one, friend, acquaintance, stranger, as you would like to be treated, is that really so difficult? It may seem to be an impossible task; however, it is our own fearful thoughts that make it so.

There are methods for canceling out fear; one is laughter, and another is singing. They set up vibrations, which activate the cells of our body. The one sure method is trusting in God. Daily prayer and communion with God, asking for guidance and wisdom, will bring peace and harmony to one's body and life. Health follows naturally when we are happy. I am sure we can testify to the fact that when fearful we feel tired, run down, and nervous. However, when we laugh, sing, love, and trust, all positive feelings, fear is eliminated.

That is the one emotion which robs us of life. The more fear the less life, until fear brings about the state we call death.

God did not create man to die. If this were so, than it would be better for us to die in infancy and not live in a material world. If Spiritual Law did not govern us, and if death were a part of God's plan, then every time we tried to heal the sick, and cure the infirmed, we would be defying the Law. God's Law is Life, abundant, unlimited!

It is becoming more and more apparent that Life is eternal, especially to those who have had 'life after death' experiences. If you have read <u>Life After Life</u> and <u>Reflections On Life After Life</u> by Dr. Moody, you know from the interviews that the crossover from the visible to the invisible is full of light, peace, warmth, and beauty. It is an experience of ongoing, not an ending.

Life is! The release of this mortal shell is nothing more than a continuance of growth and learning. It is passing from one grade to another; it is going to a new room at the old school. We have visited the school before, and now that we have learned what was necessary in this lifetime, take leave of the old and put on the new. We return and advance. Each time we leave, we move upward to another grade to attain more knowledge. There is nothing to fear, for in knowledge, there is Truth, in Truth, there is love, and in love, there is fulfillment of being.

Man was not born to die, neither was he born to fear. Cleanse your consciousness of fear, and the idea of the finality of death. Allow yourself to experience the fullness of a rich and abundant life.

Judas is the disciple who represents Life. Life must be guided divinely and expressed rightfully, and though he can be a betrayer, is capable of redemption. Judas governs the sensations of the body which can betray the body if used wrongly. Indulgence of any kind is harmful, and to redeem the greedy part of Judas is to cleanse oneself of self-gratification.

Embrace Eternal Life, my friends, as you embrace a birth. I will leave you this morning with a selected reading that I frequently perform at a Unity Memorial service. May it give you peace, and a new outlook on a former misconception.

There Is No Death

I am standing on the seashore. A ship at my side spreads her white sails to the morning breeze and starts for the blue ocean. She is an object of beauty and strength, and I stand and watch her until at length she is a speck of white cloud just where the sea and sky come to mingle with each other.

Then someone at my side says, "There! She's gone!" Gone where? Gone from my sight, that is all. She is just as large in mast, hull, and spar as she was when she left my side, and she is just as able to bear her load of living weight to her destined harbor.

Her diminished size is in me, not in her. And just at that moment when someone at my side says, "There! She's gone!" There are other eyes watching her coming, and other voices ready to take up the glad shout, "There she comes!"

And that dear ones, is dying.

Taken from a Unity pamphlet

May God Bless you in wisdom and understanding!

PART THREE

CHAPTER XXII:
Holidays

Holidays are a very significant part of our lives. In reliving them some of us will smile at the sweet poignant memories while others will sadly focus on difficult ones. As children, we remember the delicious smells and the activity surrounding the event, not only the preparation, but also the welcoming of family and friends around the Thanksgiving Day table.

The variety of food and the delicious desserts that graced the table gave rise to further excitement. Then just four weeks later, although to a child it is an eternity, there is Christmas, and all anticipation culminates on that special day of joy. When we are mature adults, the holidays are still important. However, from the time we sit at the Thanksgiving Day table until we open the gifts Christmas morning, there is an underlying stress. The stress of buying, preparing, issuing invitations, deciding what gifts to get and then wrapping them, decorating the house and tree, and still having enough energy to prepare the holiday meal. Nevertheless, we do it because there is something compelling about getting together with friends and family (no matter how dysfunctional) and sharing the ups, and sometimes downs, with those we love.

We cannot forget Easter. It may not cause the hullabaloo the other two holidays do, but there is some preparation and expense, especially the Easter outfits. At least that is the way it was in my day. On that morning, everything was brand new from our underwear out. After church, we paraded around in our finery and felt like 'Mrs. Astor's pet horse.' (Forgive me for showing my age with that simile.)

For the minister, Christmas and Easter are the busiest times of the year, not only for the reasons above, but it is a time of teaching, renewing, and instilling in consciousness, what the specific holidays mean to us Spiritually.

Joanne M. Dator

I thought it would be fitting to end the book with several holiday messages given over the years.

CHAPTER XXIII:
ENTER HIS GATES WITH THANKSGIVING

Good Morning and a Happy Thanksgiving to you all!

In my formative years, I attended a Baptist church, and every Sunday morning we would end the service with the hymn, "Praise God from Whom All Blessings Flow." Unity has modified the words to "Praise God That Good Is Everywhere" and it continues…

"Praise to the love we all may share; the life that thrills through you and me;

Praise to the Truth that sets us free".

When we praise God, the words we use expand our own God-awareness. This allows the movement of God to flow through us. We know praise works wonders because praise works on everything and everyone-animals, plants, strangers, even enemies. Praise a small child and see the glow spread across his face. Did you know you could praise your abilities? When you do, your brain cells expand and increase in capacity and intellect. When we speak words of encouragement and appreciation, they quicken the mind, which creates a magnet that attracts good. Therefore, it stands to reason the more we praise God the more good will unfold in our lives, and the more we give thanks, the more we will have to be thankful for.

The true message of the Spiritual teaching of Unity is to help us, as individuals, to "know thyself." Its purpose is not to teach us more about Jesus, although our teachings are based on His teachings, nor to teach us according to <u>man's</u> word what God is. Unity's purpose is to bring forth a desire within to know who and what we are, our purpose here on earth, and most importantly, our relationship to God, and to the man called Jesus. It is the desire of Unity teachers and ministers that you discover this Truth for yourself by going within and listening to the still small voice for guidance and wisdom.

The church building in and of itself is not important. What is important is that people of like minds come together to unite. There are many who claim they do not like organized church. I believe this is just another barrier, or excuse, used by those who are afraid to 'hear', or do not have faith in their beliefs. There is only one way for us to come into the realization, or the Truth of our being and that is by going within and seeking. However, everyone needs motivation, and that is the reason for a church building. It is a place where we can come together, make a joyful noise, share our thoughts and experiences, and prayerfully, raise not only our own consciousness, but also those whom we befriend.

When we think of God, we are praying. When we think of love, we are praying. When we give thanks, we are praying. Prayer is not something we do <u>for</u> God; it is something we do for ourselves. It should never be a means to placate, implore, or plead. Prayer is the way we discover we are, in reality, praying to ourselves, not the human body, but to the Spiritual part, the God within. Eric Butterworth, Unity minister and one of my favorite authors wrote, "We do not pray to God, but <u>from a consciousness of God</u>." Prayer brings us higher in thought as we commune with that part of us that knows no limitation. Answered prayer does not depend on a fickle being, but in the faith/belief in our oneness of being, and the goodness thereof.

There are those who teach that in order to enter the silence, we must sit a certain way, place our hands in a certain way, take off our shoes, or lie down. There are those who would tell us what not to do. Someone told me not to meditate in the bathtub. These guidelines put limitations on meditation. What is important when entering the silence is our state of mind, a knowing 'God is everywhere present'. We can be in the middle of a busy airport, driving a car, jogging in the park, doing the dishes, or standing on our heads. If we center our minds on God, we can communicate with Him. Henry Ward Beecher said:

> "A man has a right to go to God by any way which is true to him. If you can think it out, that it your privilege. One thing is certain, the

child has a right to nestle in his father's bosom, whether he climbs upon his knee, or in the chair by the side of him. Anyway, wherever you have seen God pass, mark it and sit in that window again."

As previously stated, prayer is our means of communication with God. It is a Spiritual language, and 'true prayer', prayer that comes from the heart of a believer, is answered. Those that 'appear' not to be answered occur because we have put limitations on God. When we pray with suspicion and doubt, we express a lack of faith. God works through us to the degree <u>we allow</u>. To illustrate, electricity flows through the wires in your home; if there is a blockage, it stops flowing. Remove the blockage and it will flow freely again. Doubt is the blockage to answered prayer. Another mistake that we make is praying for something in the future. I need a job next week; I must get over this cold by Friday; I wish to meet my life-mate soon. When we ask for something to happen in the future, it delays fulfillment. Do you remember what Jesus prayed when he raised Lazarus from the dead? *Father, I thank thee that thou* <u>hast heard</u> *me, and I* <u>knew</u> *thou hearest me always,"* (John 11:41, 42) He did not ask in a pleading way, "Please raise Lazarus," He prayed knowing <u>it was already done</u>. He had faith in His Father to grant Him that which He requested.

<u>Mind is the Maker!</u> First, there is the idea then the thought and, then the demonstration. The book of Hebrews tells us, *"...so that things which are seen were not made of things which do appear"* (11:3) all things come forth from invisibility to visibility. God has bestowed His Power upon us to create. It is our responsibility to get in touch with it, feel it and, use it, not only for our good; but also for the good of mankind.

As with all of God's gifts and promises, there is a condition. We must be willing to step aside and allow, be willing to release; *"...but the Father that dwelleth in me, he doeth the works."* (John 14:10) We may sincerely say, "That's easy, I want God to have dominion," but let us take a remembrance check. How many times have you attempted to be in charge when having a 'discussion' with family or friends and have said, "No, No, this is the way we should do it." "If you go down that path, you are making a mistake." "Listen to me; I know what I'm talking about." In reality, we really do not know, and we certainly do not know what is best for someone else. There are times we do not know what is best for ourselves, for we see though human eyes and <u>judge</u>

by appearance, and appearances do lie. Each of us has an inner guide, and we listen or do not listen according to where we are on life's path.

There are those, and at times even those most devout, who for one reason or another, will not listen, or heed, the inner guidance. That, too, is a learning process. Therefore, we need to rely on our own guidance for self, and for the highest good of all concerned release others to their Higher Power.

Prayer should be happy, a time of thanksgiving, filled with feelings of love and the desire to share. When faced with an overwhelming challenge trust enough to enter into prayer, in the consciousness of, "I knew thou hearest me". Have faith; eliminate fear-the fear of losing someone you love, the fear of not having financial security, the fear of a debilitating or fatal disease. Enter into prayer confident that God is not only listening but is already fulfilling your request. This is all the assurance you need to feel life in the face of death, abundance in the appearance of lack, loved in the midst of a hateful situation. God does answer prayer.

Enter His gates with praise and thanksgiving; enter with the knowledge there is only One Presence and One Power in the universe, God the Good, Omnipotent. Jesus brought forth His Christ consciousness upon this foundation. Dear ones, you too can bring forth the same potential, the seed, the Christ, which is within you.

We deny the One Presence and Power of God when we give credence to any opposing power. This in turn makes us doubt and despair. There is only God, Omnipotent, Omniscience, Omnipresent! There is no other Power, no matter what the appearance; the Spirit of God is in the midst of you, me, all of us, in all situations.

Before I close, let me ask you, when you enter the silence are you eager? Do you feel you are coming into the Presence of Divinity? There are those who say they fall asleep or get nothing out of meditation. It is possible one's attitude is not one of complete receptivity. Imagine, if you will, how you would feel if you were going to a lecture or a concert given by someone you revered. You would enter the hall with excitement, anticipation, eager to hear this person. Your attention would be fixed and your mind alert. It is in this manner we enter the Kingdom wherein resides the Presence of God.

Therefore, our first step in quiet meditation is enthusiasm, and the second, relaxation. As long as we occupy our minds with challenges, angry thoughts, tenseness, or discomfort of any kind, we cannot be at ease. Quietly tell your body to be still, relax, (it will obey) sweep negative thoughts gently from your mind and free yourself from limitation. Allow the Spirit of God access. The last step is concentration, not fixedly to word or thought, but pleasantly turning to the nature of God, His Goodness, His Wholeness, His Presence, His love for you. There is no specific time to remain in the silence. In the beginning, if your interest span is of short duration and you achieve a feeling of peace within five or ten minutes, it is not necessary to force yourself to sit longer. You will find, as you continue the practice of meditation, you will automatically remain for longer and longer periods.

Everyday, as well as this Thanksgiving, acknowledge the good in your life. Give thanks to the Source of your being, not because God is looking for, or needs your gratitude, but it is a way to keep in mind the Goodness of God. The closer we come to know God, the more God we express; the more we express, the more good is manifested through us.

> *"Enter into His gates with thanksgiving, and into his courts with praise:"*
> (Psalm 100:4)

> *'... and thy Father which seeth in secret shall reward thee openly."* (Matthew 6:6)

Thank you for being, God bless!

CHAPTER XXIV:
GOD, MAN, SANTA CLAUS

A Very Merry Christmas to All!

As I sat at my desk, pondering a Christmas message a thought occurred to me. Could I make a correlation between, God, man, and Santa Claus? Santa Claus is a 'so-called' myth; however, the Dutch report of a man who loved children, and gave them gifts; he became the patron saint of the children, St. Nicholas. We adopted 'St. Nick' and have pictured him a jolly fat man with a long white beard, and wearing a red suit. Throughout the ages, children have loved this image just as we did when we were children.

We must be partial to long white beards because in our imagery of God, we have bestowed one on Him as well. In doing so, we have created God in <u>our</u> image. We find in Webster's dictionary, God is defined as a 'being with supreme powers'; a saint is defined a holy or godly person. My definition of Santa Claus is a good and loving being with miraculous powers. Why, because the image of Santa Claus brings joy, hope, and love to children everywhere, I also consider the "idea of Santa Claus" as a miracle worker. In my life, there were many times when obtaining a 'certain desired item' appeared impossible, either because of lack of funds, or unavailability, and then suddenly, it became possible. Therefore, I have concluded that we are saints with supreme powers, for we have, at one time or another in our lifetime, played Santa Claus, and within every one of us lives the Spirit of God.

There is a definite relationship between God and man as stated in Psalms 8: 4-8

> "*What is man, that Thou are mindful of him? and the son of man, that thou visiteth him? For thou hast made him a little lower than the angels, and hast crowned him with glory and honor. Thou madest him to have*

> *dominion over the works of Thy hands; thou hast put all things under his feet: All sheep and oxen, yea, and the beasts of the field; The fowl of the air, and the fish of the sea, and whatsoever passeth through the paths of the seas."*

What is man? Man is God's channel, His manner of expression, man made in the very image and likeness of God! Man is created a little lower than the angels, and given dominion over <u>all things</u> in the world. God has given man the power to fashion, create, and manifest. Have we not created the image of Santa Claus, and have we not mis-created the image of God? Many say they do not believe in Santa Claus; could that mean they secretly do not believe in God?

If you do not believe in Santa Claus than I feel sad, for you have lost, or maybe forgotten, the excitement of childhood. I believe in Santa Claus because for me he and God are one! Santa does not have a form, is not someone we can point to, neither does God have form nor can we point to Him. If you do believe in a manifest God, sitting on a throne, judging, and playing favorites, then let me remind you what Jesus told us, "*God is a Spirit,*" (John 4:24) <u>not form</u>. God is First Cause, He is Principle. This means He was before the world existed, and will ever be. As Principle, the absolute reality of the planet, and although formless, God is the Source from which all form appears. Charles Fillmore wrote, "as the principle of music moves through the tones, so does the principle of mind move through ideas."

God is Absolute Good, Unchanging, Eternal, and Pure. We also know the elements which make up this Good are Divine Ideas, Life, Love, Substance, and Power. We base our individual ideas of God, the duality of God, on what we heard as youngsters. Later on, we may come to question, "How can there be duality if there is only One Power?" If there comes a time when things <u>appear</u> to go wrong in our lives, and <u>we conclude,</u> "God is unloving", that is a misconception from old conditioning. God is Love and love is not responsible for problems.

Jesus taught us how to understand Principle as personal when He said to call it "Father". I am sure when Jesus gave us this image, He did not mean for us to make Him out to be a stern judge meting out rewards and judgments, nor did He mean for us to see God as male and exclude the female. God would be best described as 'it', but we are programmed to shudder at such a thought.

God is Spirit; God is Creative Energy. God does not have anything; God is everything; the total of all things whether visible or invisible. Our relationship to this Energy is simple. We, created in His image are therefore Spiritual beings. God is within every living thing, every plant, every animal, and every manifestation. All creation is from one Spirit; part of the whole is in all, just as the wave is in the ocean. We as His offspring contain part of the wholeness of God; every individual is God in expression.

In Genesis 3:21 it is written, "*Unto Adam also and to his wife did the Lord God make coats of skins, and clothed them.*" This scripture clearly tells us, God brought man into visibility; this is the first reference in the Bible of man taking form. To exist means to stand forth. Man stands forth from God! Without you, God cannot express. You are His eyes, His ears, His mouth, His hands, His legs. You are God's means of being here on earth.

Did the thought ever occur to you that God could do nothing without something to express through? God is Pure Being. God is! Therefore, there needs to be something in existence for God to think, move, and speak though, hence the creation of man. To make this clearer, let us use the example of electricity. This force runs through a building. In and of itself it does nothing, but plug an appliance into the source and power surges through it. This is our relationship to Principle; as beings, we need a source of supply for every need. Oh, I know, there are those who think they do not need anyone or anything but themselves, but are they truly happy?

On a more personal level, God could be considered not only Father, but Mother also, and we can reach, can feel, and come to know this Presence. We are co-creators with Him, and He gave us dominion over all things, the earth, our bodies, our affairs. There is no limit in God; therefore no limit to the source of our being. God, as supplier, is ready to give to us just as the electricity provides when called upon. (When we flip the switch, we are asking for it.)

"*Fear not, little flock; for it is your Father's good pleasure to give you the kingdom.*" (Luke 12:32) He will supply not only what we need but also the good we desire. He provides us with our desires because God *is* 'the desire tapping at the door of consciousness'. The desire for anything is God's promise to us that it is ours already. It is ours for the taking, and taking is realizing the law of supply and demand. If our dream was not available in the invisible realm, we could not possibly picture it. For example, I did not dream of becoming a lawyer because I did not have any desire to try cases. I could not be a businesswoman for I did not want to be in the corporate world. My desire was/is to teach, to find, and reach those who are seeking. I stand before you today doing what I know in my heart is God's desire for me.

In the truest sense, desire is man's inner response to some form of good, which is already prepared for him; desire, in itself, is always good. There are those who would disagree and pose the question, "How about 'wrong desires' such as wanting someone else's mate or lusting after someone's property or affluence?" To that I say, "There is no such thing as wrong desires only the misunderstanding of rightful ones." It is not the person or the things that motivate the desire, but the condition it represents. God wants us to have love and prosperity in all ways. The willful part of us leads us astray, that little self who wants what it sees with no regard for others. But if we have patience and faith, He will guide us to our own good without hurting others.

We speak of consciousness, sub-consciousness, and in Unity, we use the term super-consciousness. Consciousness is an awareness of what is, right now. If you look at this pulpit, and concentrate on it, you are fully aware of it. If you are not listening to me, you are fully aware of the thoughts in your mind. When you leave this building look at the sky, and see, and feel, the warmth of the sun, your consciousness filled with the beauty of what you see and feel. Life is consciousness, thoughts are things, mind is the maker, what we concentrate on is what composes our world. Too often, our thoughts are concentrated on the material world and on a life of struggle, of getting and being, no matter what the cost. However, there is another world, which you are part of, and that is the Spiritual world. It is a world of receiving; it is a world of harmony, peace, and prosperity given to you without strife. To live in that world all we need do is expand our thinking through prayer, meditation, and positive thoughts to bring us closer to God.

It mystifies me that there are those Truth seekers who realize how dis-ease is attracted, and challenges can be averted, but refuse to see that wholeness, peace, and joy can also be 'attracted' into one's life. Within you is the Power to bring forth any condition you so desire. You are a co-creator with God. God is the life force, which is ever renewing and revitalizing, if <u>we do not get in the way</u>. *"For in him we live, and move, and have our being;"* (Acts 17:28)

The key to all manifestation is faith. One must first believe in order for faith to grow and strengthen. Liken belief to the key of your ignition and faith the ignition; turn the key of belief and faith activates the power to move forward. Faith is saying 'yes' to God.

Now let us get back to our original premise. Is there a similarity between Santa Claus and God? What is your earliest recollection of Santa Claus and Christmas? Can you remember the anticipation, the excitement? I still remember how excited I got. "Where was he?" "When would he arrive at my house?" "How would he ever get into the apartment?" We had no chimney. As each day grew closer to Christmas, I knew he was coming. I had no doubts. I cannot say the same for my parents. I am sure they were worried, for we were in the midst of a depression, but as a child, the appearance of lack did not touch me, and I believed! Is there a difference between a child knowing Santa will come, and the adult knowing God is all providing; both have an unshakable faith?

Come Christmas morning, I would run into the living room, and, lo and behold, there were the presents; I felt excited and happy. Is this not the same way we feel when our Father-Mother God bestows a gift on us we so desired? The child crawls on his parents lap and asserts his belief in Santa not knowing to whom he is talking. The adult when speaking to his Creator does not know the full potential within himself, and the true relationship to whom he is speaking. Can we not become again as the little child and trust that, "God, the source of all good," will supply our every need.

This Christmas give yourself a present. Give yourself permission to stop being logical and practical; they have no place in Spirituality, instead surrender and trust.

> *"Trust in the Lord with all thine heart; and lean not unto thine own understanding.*
>
> *In all thy ways acknowledge him, and he shall direct thy paths"* (Proverbs 3:5, 6)

Remember the faith you had in Santa Claus and transfer it to God, and great shall be your reward.

Have a Merry and Joyous Christmas. God Bless!

CHAPTER XXV:
John before Jesus

Happy Holidays!

Soon Santa will visit your homes, and the excitement of the season will hit its peak. My wish for each of you; "May this excitement continue through the twelve days of Christmas and beyond."

As a child, did you ever wonder how Santa would fit or manage to get down the chimney? Worse yet, if you had no chimney, how could he get to you? I sure did, but come Christmas morning, all questions and concerns were gone, and miracle of miracles, there were all those presents under the tree. What a wonderful entity Santa was/is.

Allow me to digress for just a moment. I am so sick and tired of those who speak of 'reality' and the commercialism of Christmas for they are destroying the gift of childhood fantasies. Yes, it is true as we get older Christmas can be a time of stress, but for the children it is a time of wonder. I for one do not want to take that away from them. The very wonder and belief keep them innocent and trusting. What is reality? It is what we hold in mind as true, and if it brings joy, why the need to destroy that joy? As for the commercialism, we ourselves are at fault by adding to the frenzy of bigger and better. I wish to perpetuate the belief in "Santa Claus", although today I call him by another name. He cannot be seen, but is all seeing, and is very real to me.

> *"Verily, I say unto you, Except ye be converted, and become as little children, ye shall not enter into the kingdom of heaven."* (Matthew 18:3)

The Kingdom of Heaven, that place in consciousness where peace reigns; that place in consciousness where you accept and know; that place in consciousness where you, as a little child, are innocent, trusting, loving, accepting. I believe even the most skeptical of people have had moments when they were in 'The Kingdom'.

Think back in time and recapture the feelings you had on Christmas morning. Let them fill you and warm you. Was not the belief in Santa Claus a prelude to believing in a loving, all providing, Father-Mother God? As children, we heard, we believed, we expected. As adults, we hear, we doubt, we set aside. It is as if suddenly we have to touch God to believe He is there. Our childlike faith gives way to adult skepticism. I believe that deep within we do know God is there. We know because as we grow older, and we begin to think for ourselves, awareness begins. From deep within there is a remembrance, a knowing that, "there is a special being who loves us, who wants to see us happy, and will grant any wish we have." A warm feeling comes over me when I remember my childhood Christmases.

Santa Claus before God…John before Jesus! *"Verily, verily, I say unto thee, Except a man be born again, he cannot see the kingdom of God."* (John 3:3)

According to George Lamsa, a leading authority of the Aramaic language, the language Jesus spoke, the correct translation for the words used for '*born again*' meant, "to change one's thoughts and habits." Do you remember the story of Nicodemus? He was a prominent Pharisee, a ruler of the Jews. He spoke southern Aramaic; therefore, he did not comprehend Jesus' words. Nicodemus visited Jesus at night, for he did not want any of his peers to see him conversing with Him, and asked, "How can a man be born again?" Jesus explained that there is a Spiritual world that man is heir to and he must be reborn (change his thinking) in order to see it.

We are physical, mental, and Spiritual beings. We come into the world as physical, develop mentally into an intellectual awakening, and then there comes a time when there is a Spiritual awakening; we are born again. The authorized Bible version of born anew states, "We realize we are Spiritual beings, living in a Spiritual world, governed by Spiritual law. The physical and the intellectual process, happens naturally, but the Spiritual awakening occurs in accordance with our free choice, and comes from earnest desire. It is up to each individual to take the initiative because Spiritual birth is never forced."

There was a priest whose name was Zacharias; his wife's name was Elizabeth. They were two very good people who revered God and lived by His law. There was one shadow in their lives, however; they did not have sons. This was Zachariah and Elizabeth's dream and they wanted very much to fulfill that dream. She felt guilty and had long since passed childbearing age. During the holy days, Zacharias went to the temple to pray and minister to the people; when it became his turn, he went in to burn incense. While he was praying, an angel of the Lord came upon him. Zacharias became frightened and the angel said,

> *"...Fear not, Zacharias: for thy prayer is heard; and thy wife Elizabeth shall bear thee a son, and thou shalt call his name John. ...and many shall rejoice at his birth. For he shall be great in the sight of the Lord;... and he shall be filled with the Holy Ghost, even from his mother's womb. And many of the children of Israel shall he turn to the Lord their God."* (Luke 1:13-16)

As usual when the one thing we have asked for and desired and gratification is within reach, we question and doubt. Zacharias was no exception to human emotion. He told the angel it was impossible, he was too old, and his wife could no longer bear children. The angel then said because he doubted, and did not accept God's word, *"And, behold, thou shalt be dumb, and not able to speak, until the day that these things shall be performed,"* (Luke 1:20)

Six months later, in Nazareth, an angel appeared to Elizabeth's cousin, Mary. She heard of Elizabeth's pregnancy, and that she too, would conceive a child, and his name would be Jesus. Mary went to stay with her cousin, and when John was born there was great rejoicing. At the naming of the child, Zacharias speech returned, and there was a realization among the town's people that this truly was an exceptional child!

John's story is important historically, but it is a more important one for our spiritual growth. John was born of unusual circumstances; he grew and waxed strong in Spirit. He stayed apart and dedicated himself to God. He lived in the desert until the day he appeared in Israel. John did not dress as the men of the times, and it is thought this was done to remind them of the prophesy of Elijah's return. When he began preaching, his message was far different from that of Jesus. He proclaimed the coming of the Messiah, but felt it would be a time of terror rather than rejoicing. John would shout, *"Repent ye; for the kingdom of heaven is at hand."* (Matthew 3:2) He claimed severe punishment for wrong doers, and only those who were truly righteous would be safe. John's message, "repent or else."

There came a time when John was put in prison because of his radical preaching. He waited expectantly for Jesus to come and save him. When this did not occur, he began to doubt. "Was he wrong? Was Jesus really the Messiah?" John was tempted to the point of abandoning his proclamations. He sent messengers to find Jesus and ask Him if He were the one, or if there was another. Jesus' answer was neither yes, or no. Instead, He continued to heal the sick, make well the lame, and restore sight to the blind. After awhile, He told the messengers to return to John, tell him what they had witnessed, and that John should decide for himself if Jesus was the Messiah.

How many times have we been in a prison of our own making? We cry out for God to save us, and when the saving does not take place immediately, we doubt it ever will. We seek answers from friends, counselors, sometimes-even strangers, and all the time, the answers lie within our own realization.

On the surface, it may seem as if there was no significant teaching or connection between John the Baptist, Jesus the Christ, and us, but let us look at what each means and stands for metaphysically.

John the Baptist signifies a high intellectual perception of Truth; however, one not quickened by Spirit. By that I mean, he knows in his head but does not feel in his heart. He represents an attitude of mind, which is eager for the rule of Spirit. This attitude, itself, is not spiritual but has Spiritual possibilities. This attitude sees evil as a reality because it has not come to the realization that the appearance of evil <u>is temporary and not of God</u>. It seeks to do right, but is crude and cries out in the wilderness. At the first encounter John had with Jesus, he said, *"This is he of whom I said, After me cometh a man which is preferred before me: for he was before me."* (John 1:30)

John, who represents the intellect, comes first in consciousness. Spiritual awareness, represented by Jesus, comes forth after the consciousness awakens; it is always there just not realized. The intellect must make way for the Spirit. There comes a time when we cannot, must not, rationalize or look to appearances, but accept and know there is a Higher Law, which rules us; another world that we cannot see, feel, touch, but will come to know just as strongly as we know this one.

Santa Claus before God; the one in the red suit, who teaches us the joy of giving and receiving. It is this image that stirs up emotions within, and brings forth feelings of warmth and love into conscious realization. It helps us to know 'faith does the work'. As the belief in Santa Claus diminishes, the faith in <u>God</u> grows. Childhood imaginings develop into adult manifestations. We feel God's Presence within; we witness His Good and share it with all.

John before Jesus; the man who intuitively knew he was the forerunner. The man who declared, *"He must increase, but I must decrease."* (John 3:30) In order for the awareness of Spirit, the Christ, to take hold, we release the intellect. We let go and let God.

Thoreau said, "As long as man stands in his own way, everything seems to be in his way." How true. We ask for healing, and then concentrate on pain; we ask for prosperity, and then complain we have not enough; we want harmonious relationships, and then pick a fight or respond in anger to loved ones. We want to be Spiritual but claim limitation, and when the things we pray for do not materialize 'yesterday', we lose faith.

Today, with all our intellectual growth, we know everything about what goes on around us but practically nothing about ourselves. The human being's biggest problem is separation from God. The 'lost soul' is the soul that has lost sight of God's Omnipresence; does not hold in mind, "Wherever I am, God is." The found soul, the aware soul says, "God is in the midst of this situation."

God is Ever-Present, Loving, Giving, and Living through His creations. We must know and feel 'God and I are one.' We, created in His image are Spiritual Beings. We are His way of expressing. He has given us the power to manifest His goodness. When we identify with God, it takes nothing from Him for He is Almighty; neither does it take away from, nor diminish an individual, rather it enhances us as it builds character, increases our personality, and gives us a joy for living.

In closing, I would ask you to listen, and hear these words as if God were speaking to you now…

"My child, I sent your brother to tell you that you may have life and live it abundantly. It is <u>my</u> desire that you live life to the fullest with every joy and happiness, for that is what you deserve. I created for you a world of good. However, you chose to see a world of evil; a world of worry, tension, upset. You think you have to fight just to stay afloat, because you believe you are living in a material world, governed by intellect, and as a result, you close yourself off from me. Hear Me now. You are My offspring, you are a Spiritual Being, your true world is Spiritual, and is governed by Spiritual Law, My law. <u>I love you;</u> I will always protect and provide for you."

Joanne M. Dator

Christ, the Spirit within, can prove who and what we are when we behead the consciousness of John the Baptist; when we allow the intellect to diminish and the awareness of Spirit to increase. God has promised us that we will partake of His Divine Nature and escape the limitations of the world.

Let us accept our innate divinity as we accepted Santa Claus on Christmas morning. Let us look forward to answered prayers with the same enthusiasm we had when we looked for our presents under the tree. Let the light of Spiritual awareness burn as brightly within, as the lights on our trees burn without.

God bless you, and have a very blessed Christmas.

CHAPTER XXVI:
THE VIRGIN BIRTH

A very Blessed Christmas to each of you!

Christmas is upon us again, and as a woman, I can easily equate these weeks proceeding the holiday, to those before giving birth, the heaviness, the weariness, but, at the same time anticipation and eagerness for the day to arrive.

Jesus, the baby, the boy, the man, was a human being. I am sure He lived His early years much the same as any little boy. It was in adulthood, after much study, and introspection, He achieved what is possible for everyone, Christ consciousness. The Christ is the Spiritual part within each of us; it is that which makes us one with God. That part of us has the same attributes, the same likeness, and the same power as our Creator. Physically, Jesus was as you and me; mentally; however, He saw with a clearer vision. He looked beyond the physical. He looked to a truer reality. This made Him appear to be different, but in Truth, it was His knowledge, application, and faith in the <u>Truth of his being</u>, that made it so.

In the Old Testament book of Isaiah, it is prophesied:

"The people that walked in darkness have seen a great light: they that dwell in the land of the shadow of death, upon them the light has shined." (9:2)

"For unto us a child is born, unto us a son is given: and the government shall be upon his shoulder: and his name shall be called Wonderful, Counselor, The mighty God, The everlasting Father, The Prince of Peace." (9:6)

A child born to the people who were filled with worry, doubt, and walked in fear, to them this child would bring recognition, acceptance, and awakening. They would be filled with illumination, the light of Spiritual knowledge. That child was Jesus, son of Joseph and Mary. He went through all the mental and physical phases we all do. He experienced trials and temptations but did not fall under the dominion of evil thoughts; He overpowered them.

We accept the account of the Virgin Birth; however, not once was it openly talked about, or discussed during Jesus' ministry. Contrary to what other religions state, Unity <u>does</u> accept the Virgin Birth, and finds it to have great metaphysical significance. It appears to be a miraculous event; however, we, as Truth students, recognize Spiritual law transcends material law and things, which are impossible to man-are possible with God. Mary was not only a virgin because of her physical state, but because of her mental state. She was pure in mind and heart. It is from that, we derive the symbolic meaning of the birth.

Within each of us lies the seed of perfection, the Christ, the son of God. It begins its growth within individual consciousness, as we cleanse our minds and hearts from the human thought of limitation and negativity.

Jesus, known as the carpenter, the teacher, but He was not known as one born miraculously. Remember when Jesus went back to Nazareth; the people crowded around him. *"And they said, Is not this Jesus, the son of Joseph, whose father and mother we know? How is it then he saith, I came down from heaven?"* (John 6:42) This clearly shows that the people of his own village did <u>not</u> know, or believe, in the miracle of his birth.

I believe Jesus was no different from you or I; He was tempted, hungered, thirsted, became angry, and wept over the death of a loved one. He asked us to follow him, to believe in His words. *"Verily, verily, I say unto you, He that believeth on me, the works that I do he shall do also; and greater works than these shall he do;"* (John 14: 12) It could not be clearer; keep to his teaching, above all have faith, and in doing so, <u>we would do what he did and even greater</u>. He would never have promised that if it were not true. Contained within the statement is the acknowledgment that He was <u>not</u> different from us. Jesus emphasized repeatedly that God was/is <u>our</u> Father; we are all one. For us to think He is Divine, solely on the reports of His conception, keeps us separated from Him, from his teaching, and most importantly, from God.

The Virgin birth gives us another important lesson:

Though Christ a thousand times in Bethlehem be born,

If He is not born in thee, the soul is forlorn.

Liken the Christ-the spirit of God within-to an embryo waiting to be born in a virgin state of mind. A pure mind, one that affirms only good; one which puts God first, and permits 'God's will be done'. You see we must give permission because God gave us free will to choose what path we would travel, and by what means we would use to accomplish our destination. He also promised not to interfere with the choices we make <u>unless</u> we asked for help.

Taking in other aspects of the birth, the scripture does not go into how many Wise men there were; therefore, the number is not a fact. The idea seems to have come about during the fifth century because of the three gifts. Later on another writer decided the Wise men were Kings coming to pay homage to the King of Kings. It was in the eighth century that they were given names, Kaspar, Belshazzar, and Melchior; however, there is <u>no</u> verification of any of this in scripture. Metaphysically, there <u>is</u> a teaching in their visit. Wise men are forever searching for the Christ. These men represent the wisdom that is within the soul from the beginning of time. Coming from the east signifies 'from within' or inner consciousness. Those searching for the Christ can find Him by going within.

Let us examine the significance of the star. There are some claims that it was a periodic appearance of Haley's comet. However, consider this: if the star was shining so brilliantly in the sky, why did Herod and his followers <u>not</u> see it? The Wise men had stopped for directions to the babe's location, and Herod asked them to notify him when they found the baby, and to let him know His whereabouts. When they did not return with the information, Herod had all the boy babies under two slain. There was this brilliant light shining in the sky, and no one saw it but the Wise Men and the shepherds. The star metaphysically means; <u>Spiritual things must be spiritually discerned</u>. The Wise Men were spiritually illumined, and therefore, were able to see the guiding star. Herod and the unillumined saw nothing. By the way, Herod stands for the ruling will, or ego. When the personal ego takes over; we are led by fear, jealousy, and cruelty, which can become destructive. Personal will can kill every good thought, every good purpose, arising in consciousness; hence, the slaying of the infants.

I mentioned the shepherds; what lesson do we learn from them? When we carefully shepherd our thoughts, there will come to us moments of spiritual illumination that will guide and direct us to the Christ (child.) However, the shepherds went even further. They said, *"…Let us go now even unto Bethlehem, and see this thing which is come to pass,"* (Luke 2:15) they not only heard the angelic chorus, and saw the light of the star, but they went to Bethlehem. They heard; they saw; and they followed; they made contact with the Christ.

Believing in the Virgin Birth is not the key to understanding; understanding the Virgin Birth is the key to Spirit. Truth is within all. It matters not how Jesus was born, what matters is His way of life. He gave instruction on how to live life, all we need do is follow those instructions to open great and new avenues some of which you would not dare to dream.

The scriptures refer to 'our being heirs.' Paul wrote to the Romans, *"The Spirit itself beareth witness with our spirit, that we are the children of God; And if children, then heirs; heirs of God, and joint-heirs with Christ;"* (8:16, 17)

This is the Truth of you! Every one of us <u>is</u> God's child. We are joint heirs with Christ. Now is the time to realize, and know, the Truth of your being. With God as Creator, as Father, He is your source, the One and only source of all good. He is 'sufficiency in all things'. This is the season to commit, to *"Trust in the Lord with all thine heart; and lean not unto thine own understanding. In all thy ways acknowledge him, and he shall direct thy paths"* (Proverbs 3:5, 6); and then rest, rest in the joy and comfort of His guidance and protection.

It is time to realize Jesus was not different from the rest us, and it is possible to achieve the level of Spirituality that He did. It was the Divine Origin within that He discovered, that gave Him the Power, not the circumstances of his conception. Every human being, whether aware or not, is a Divine Child of The Most High; heir to all the Father has. Our relationship to God is the same as Jesus' relationship to God.

On the earthly plane, the relationships of siblings to their parents are the same; parent to child. What gives the appearance of differences is the <u>attitude</u> of one to another; (one feeling more love/acceptance than another does) therefore, what makes Jesus the Christ appear different from us? It was His awareness of His relationship to the Father, and His strong faith in God's Love. How much are we aware, how much do we accept our relationship to God, and how unshakable is our faith? In our quest for spirituality, I would venture to guess that acceptance has the edge because if we become aware but do not allow knowledge to embrace us, awareness is left waiting for action.

The world is more and more competitive. Everyone is out to win; everyone is striving to excel. One day, I realized I was trying to compete with God. I was allowing my ego to control my personal thoughts and opinions. I needed to let go, release <u>my</u> way, what I thought was important, and allow God to work in and through me. I do not know about you, but there have been times when I insisted on doing and saying things that down deep I knew were wrong, but pushed blindly ahead anyway, only to fall flat on my face. It was then I knew it was time for a change.

Christmas is a time of joy; when joyous, we are happy, we feel free and are excited. *"Come unto me, all ye that labor and are heavy laden, and I will give you rest."* (Matthew 11:28) His promise; His arms outstretched, His presence available, it is all up to us to *"...chose you this day whom ye will serve...."* (Joshua 24:15)

We create our own worlds, and we have every opportunity to awaken to the Truth of our being. We are Spiritual beings! The birth of the Christ child takes place within the virgin territory of a pure, willing, acceptable mind. This Christmas season look about you and see love in the eyes of your children, goodness in your friends, and neighbors, forgive a loved one's harsh word that may have hurt you. I ask you to dismiss from your mind any belief you may have in the <u>power</u> of dis-ease, lack, limitation, and any fear that is lurking there. As heirs, there is no need to live under those conditions.

I leave you this morning with a beautiful message found in *A Course in Miracles* "Forget not, once this journey is begun the end is certain. Doubt along the way will come, and go, and go, to come again. You belong to Him who loves you, as He loves himself. Be not afraid. We only start again an ancient journey long ago begun, that but seems new. What is here begun, will grow in life, and strength, and hope, until the world is still an instant, and forgets all that the dream of sin has made of it. Let us go out and meet the new born world, knowing that Christ has been reborn in it, and that the holiness of this birth, will last forever. We have lost our way but He has found it for us. Let us go and bid Him welcome who returns to us to celebrate salvation and the end of all we thought we made. The morning star of this new day looks on a different world where God is welcome and His Son is with Him."

Have a very Merry Christmas and know God is blessing you now!

CHAPTER XXVII:
ENTER JERUSALEM

Good Morning!

This being Palm Sunday, I would ask you to take a mental trip with me to a city called Jerusalem. In Abraham's time, this holy city was known as Salem, later to be known as Jebus, and in Joshua's time, it became Jerusalem. The name means 'habitation of peace, abode of prosperity'. In Revelations, it symbolically means, 'the redeemed state of man'. Where is this Jerusalem? Metaphysically, it is located within; it is the place, in consciousness, where Spiritual peace resides.

We have studied men and women who have changed the course of history; however, Jesus changed the course of the world, and it was his last week on earth, which accomplished the most change. There were five things that Jesus did that angered the authorities, so much so, that they decided they had to get rid of him. What were they?

1. He cast out evil spirits from the afflicted man.

2. He dined without washing, a meaningful custom.

3. He set aside restrictions on what a Jew should eat.

4. He healed a woman on the Sabbath <u>and the most outrageous</u>

5. He raised Lazarus from the dead.

That was the last straw. You see, the Pharisees were afraid, if they allowed 'this man' to continue to perform these miracles, more and more would come to believe Him, and eventually follow Him. If that happened, the Romans would come and destroy what they, the priests, considered 'their holy place.'

Is this not typical of the hypocrite who puts more value on the outer? Those who proclaim a strong faith, but when put to a test, retreat? The Jewish nation was a great nation. The Jewish people were holy, but the leaders were afraid. Why risk it all on the doings of one man? It did not matter to them that this man was fulfilling <u>every</u> law in the scriptures. In their blind fear, they decided He must die.

As Jesus continued to travel to different areas with His message, there were warnings that Herod was after Him. They emphasized His danger, but Jesus said He would continue to do his work of teaching and healing. He also informed them that they need not worry, *"....for it cannot be that a prophet perish out of Jerusalem."* (Luke 13:33)

Take a moment to think about what this means. Jesus had a choice. He had the option to say yea, or nay; all He had to do was stay out of Jerusalem. He knew; He <u>knew</u> not even His disciples, His beloved friends who had been with Him for three years, understood who He was, or His mission. If He fled now, all would be lost, and in time forgotten. If forgotten, no one would know the joy, love, fulfillment, and the peace available in finding "oneness with God". He would make His enemies happy in retreating to Nazareth, but his purpose on earth and the message to the people would not be heard. He would become another minor prophet. The day came when he made his choice; it was time to go to Jerusalem. This man so full of compassion, love, and wisdom, knew what was to come, knew what their reaction would be, and how the attitude would change from joy to rage. He was alone, surrounded by many. Jesus entered the city that day not to fulfill his human nature, but to carry out his divine purpose.

Can you visualize the arrival, the throngs full of anticipation, and the shouts of joy? Here was their King. They spread their coats, waved palms, and shouted 'Hosanna'.

In the scriptures it says, Jesus rode in on an ass-a colt, wild, and untrained. The characteristic of such an animal is stubbornness, persistence, and endurance. Therefore, we could suppose, it would not respond favorably to anyone riding it for the first time, or to the noise and confusion. Metaphysically, this is significant. To ride means to make obedient to ones will. Jesus riding the ass symbolizes mastery of the Christ, Spiritual nature, over the animal or human nature. The people, (metaphysically), represent our thoughts, which recognize the importance of the event, and fall into place, singing Hosanna, meaning 'save now'. In other words, there is a change from personal will to 'thy will' as they look with wonder upon this gentle man.

The procession continues to the temple, and the huge crowd disperses. Jesus enters and heals those who seek him out. The scribes, and the priests, become angry for those who stayed behind are continuing to cry out, 'Hosanna to the son of David'. You see, this was the same as proclaiming him the Messiah. The priests accuse Jesus and ask, *"Hearest thou what they say?"* and He answers them, *"Yea,...Out of the mouth of babes and sucklings thou hast perfected praise."* (Matthew 21:16) Those who have 'child-like faith' support Spiritual Truth.

Before that day, Jesus had spent the week in Bethany, four miles from Jerusalem, and everyday they would walk to the holy city. It was on that Monday, as they were walking, Jesus said He was hungry, and seeing a fig tree full of leaves, went to retrieve the fruit.

When a fig tree is full of fruit the leaves are abundant; however, when they came to it, it was barren. It is here that scripture says, Jesus cursed the tree, by saying *"...Let no fruit grow on thee henceforth forever."* (Matthew 21:19) The tree withered! One commentary calls this an acted parable. There would be no reason to believe that Jesus, and his disciples, had not eaten breakfast before leaving the house that morning. Therefore, His words are symbolic. The tree stands for the Jewish nation, the leaves-the great profession of righteousness and faith.

As individuals, how can we interpret this? The barren tree stands for unfruitful conditions in one's life. We need to bring forth the fruits of our Spiritual nature, and when a certain state of mind is not constructive, we must learn to wither/withdraw any barren/sterile thoughts, and negative appearances. It is time to turn to God, have faith in a Higher Power, and become free.

Whatever the interpretation consider this: Those who proclaim their righteousness by saying, "I am a good Christian," "I believe in Jesus Christ," "I do God's Will," and then commence to criticize, condemn, and judge others; those that appear to wear their religion as a shroud, do they live it? Are they not fooling themselves, in their actions, are they any better then the Pharisees?

Another event, which took place that week, was the Last Supper. It was Thursday, now referred to as Maudy Thursday, and the last time Jesus and His disciples would eat together. While they sat at the table Jesus took the bread, broke it, and said, *"This is my body which is given for you: this do in remembrance of me."* (Luke 22; 19) In like manner, He took the cup and said, *"This cup is the new testament in my blood: this do ye, as oft as ye drink it, in remembrance of me."* (1 Corinthians 11:25)

It is a fact that the food we eat and the liquids we drink affect our flesh and blood. To eat and drink, is to appropriate, to take in, which then nourishes our bodies and becomes a part of our physical life. However, Jesus always talked about our Spiritual life and emphasized, God is Spirit. Since He spoke symbolically, the message of the Last Supper is thus; the <u>bread</u>, or body of Christ, represents <u>Substance;</u> the living <u>energy</u> out of which everything manifests. The <u>wine,</u> or the blood of Christ, represents the <u>Life</u> of Spirit. What we eat and drink nourishes our body, on the physical plane; what we think and feel nourishes our Spiritual body. As we appropriate (take in) Spiritual ideas, as we think and feel positively, stressing more good not only in our lives, but also in those around us, our thoughts and feelings become a part of our mental life.

I digress; we began this morning on a journey to Jerusalem where there is feasting signifying a receptive state of mind to all good. Jesus riding triumphantly into Jerusalem symbolizes our coming into a peaceful state of consciousness, one that is dynamic, joyous and active.

Did you ever consider that to achieve peace involves adventure? At one time or another, each of us has heard a voice, had an urge or a desire, to take a chance, to explore other possibilities. This may be surprising, but this is a prompting from within to bring us into a higher understanding. It is an idea or desire, whether mental or physical, to place us on another path. When the desire beckons, we hide from it thinking it is too hard, too risky, fear sets in, and we disregard it. The fear of ridicule, and failure, which stem from looking at appearances, makes us doubt and hesitate. You may believe it or not, but answering the call brings peace because it brings with it a feeling of excitement that escalates as we begin to consider the possibilities. You see, peace is the opposite of restlessness, which stems from boredom. When we heed the desire, listen to the still small voice that beckons, it gives us a wonderful feeling of action. It is in the doing that one feels alive.

Asking, listening, and looking for guidance from a Higher Source will bring adventures, which lead to the peace we seek. It is a peace that only God can give, and will fill us with satisfaction. Contented, we live in a consciousness of love, a love that is productive for the greater good of all.

There is a way to enter Jerusalem. It is the way of the Christ, the pathway of complete faith in our own spirituality. We begin by curtailing our fears, not looking at appearances, by looking for the good everywhere present, by blessing what we already have, and expect to have, by being more adventurous. As we identify more with the Christ within, and *use our "I Am" (our spiritual name) positively, it becomes easier to enter the habitation of peace, Jerusalem.

> * I AM strong!
>
> *I AM healthy!
>
> *I AM intelligent!
>
> *I AM prosperous in all ways!
>
> *I AM ONE WITH GOD!

God blesses you now!

Taken from <u>The Week That Changed The World</u> by Ernest C. Wilson

CHAPTER XXVIII:
Christ is Risen

Good Morning on this glorious Easter Morn:

"Christ the Lord is risen today, Alleluia!

Raise your joys and triumphs high, Alleluia!"

He lives, praise God, He lives! We shout, and sing, and cry for joy; however, do we fully realize the miracle this statement proclaims? Those of us who are into Truth teachings, those who are searching, those who would demonstrate more goodness in their lives have been taught the key is forgiveness and love, and yet, we center our thoughts, emotions, and religious teachings, on the gruesome details of the death of Jesus. The crucifix has become not only the symbol of Christianity, but also a symbol of suffering. Did you know in the Aramaic language, the language that Jesus spoke, the word used and later translated to mean suffer also means, "to allow"? To me, this means Jesus gave His permission (mentally/spiritually) for this last demonstration on the earth plane to prove His greatest Truth-Eternal Life!

There is a story written by Arnold J. Toynbee the famous historian:

"An English family lived in China and hired a Chinese lady to take care of their children. When the woman first entered their house, she appeared to be upset, and as time elapsed, she became more distressed. They would ask her what was wrong, but she seemed to be afraid to say. Finally, one day, she could not contain herself any longer, and said, there was something she could not understand. "You are good people, you love your children, and provide very well for them, and yet in every room of the house, even on the staircase, <u>I see reproductions of a criminal being put to death by some horrible torture</u> that we have never heard of here in China. I do not understand how, you loving and responsible parents can expose your children to the dreadful effects of seeing that picture, at this, the most impressionable time of their lives."

Doesn't that give one something to think about? If we knew nothing about the Christian Bible and Jesus, and saw pictures and sculptors of a man hanging on a cross, would we not question?

Paul said, "*For now we see through a glass, darkly*;" (1 Corinthians 13:12) How true, we have been looking through blinded eyes, however, seeing through the eyes of the Chinese woman, how revealing. The cross has become a symbol of unjust punishment, and to use it as an emblem of Christianity, Love and Forgiveness, is to deny the teachings of Jesus the Christ. Yes, I wear a cross, but I will not wear one with the figure of Jesus on it. To me the cross signifies freedom, life, the crossing out of negativity and coming into the light of understanding.

We revile and denounce Judas Iscariot for his act of "betrayal," yet we do not condemn Peter who also betrayed Jesus. Judas linked with the most despicable act, so much so that Dante in his writings made him lowest of all men. Christians have called Judas a murderer as if he drove the spikes and nails into the body of Jesus himself.

In reality, Judas was one of Jesus' closest friends. Jesus believed in him, picked him because He knew Judas would be a great help to them, knew he was a strong man of vision and dedication, and would sacrifice anything for a dream. That was Judas' crime. He was neither selfish nor ambitious. In fact, if you remember it was John and James who fought over who would sit at the right hand of Jesus when they entered the Kingdom.

Judas was educated, their treasurer, and had a good business head. They lived together three years and no one suspected Judas when Jesus spoke of betrayal. Another point, although Peter had had some insight as to Jesus' identity, none of the disciples fully realized His true mission, "to deliver to the masses the message of our divinity". It was not, as so many thought, to overthrow the government. Mistakenly, every one expected a political overthrow.

Not only do we not judge Peter his betrayal, but what about the other ten? They all remained quiet. Is that not the same as betrayal? They thought <u>if</u> He were divine, He would save himself. Nonetheless, we choose to blame Judas because in his zeal for his master's success he believed he would expedite the overthrow by giving Jesus the push needed to bring forth the new kingdom. Judas had no doubt that Jesus would save Himself.

It is written in the account of the Last Supper, "Satan entered into him" Satan, the negative part of human consciousness; what we today call the ego, that part within us that is concerned with superiority and selfishness, took over his will. We all have a Judas trait within us, and it is a very real influence. We believe in Spirit, but desire things of the flesh. We are divine in potential, but act human. We frustrate that potential and betray the Christ within for gratification of human desire. That day Judas fulfilled his duty, as did Jesus of Nazareth.

Jesus was a human being who awakened to His Spiritual identity; He embodied 'The Christ.' Paul describes him, *"…; but was in all points tempted like as we are, yet without sin."* (Hebrews 4:15) He was without sin not because he could not, but because He would not. Keep in mind, when one sins he mistakenly separates from good, or God. Jesus never separated Himself from God. He knew, He stated, *"I and my Father are one."* (John 10:30) *"…; but the Father that dwelleth in me, He doeth the works."* (John 14:10) He proved what he believed and knew to be true that with God all things are possible. His return from the "dead" was the final lesson.

What is the great message of Easter? First, and foremost, that Life is Eternal and you, dear one, are divine. <u>You are the very expression of God.</u> *"Verily, verily, I say unto you, He that believeth on me,* (The Christ, The I AM indwelling) *the works that I do he shall do also; and greater works than these shall he do; because I go unto my Father."* (John 14:12) Because I, Jesus the man, have made the breakthrough, the knowledge of Spiritual Oneness, you can believe in your divinity. It is your inheritance, eternal, ageless, whole, and complete. It is perfect even though the outer expression may appear imperfect. It is always strong and fearless in the face of fear and doubt. It is with you in your loneliest hours. It can never be hurt, sick, or afraid, for it is your God-self.

We cannot see God with our physical eyes, but we can feel Its Presence, know His Strength, and experience Her love. We can dwell in the consciousness of Spirit, and allow the cells of our bodies to recharge and renew, and experience healing power of wholeness; we can transcend time and know all things are possible. No matter what challenges may befall us, we can be aware of this Truth, *"Ye are of God, little children, and have overcome them: <u>because greater is He that is in you, than he that is in the world</u>."* (1 John 4:4)

"And when they looked, they saw that the stone was rolled away:" (Mark 16:4) The problems that loom large in our lives are as the stone placed in front of the tomb. If we look to God, the stone (the problems and challenges in life) shall be rolled away; however, if we continue to look at the stone, it grows in size and becomes impossible to move.

"Woman, why weepest thou? whom seekest thou?" (John 20:15) When we are in a panic, fearful, we fail to see. Mary was searching for her Lord, and He was standing right beside her. There are times we get ourselves in difficult situations because we become angry with a loved one, have a falling out with a coworker, lose a friend, a job, we become confused, irritable, lost. We forget our true reality, and get lost in appearances. Remember, turn to your "I AM", the Christ, and the Spirit within will uplift and correct all mistakes in judgment. Every time we realize and associate with our Oneness with God, a resurrection takes place, and we escape the tomb of despair.

When Mary finally realized she was looking at her Master, she ran to tell the disciples, and guess what; they did not believe her! Jesus appeared to two more disciples, and they still did not believe He was alive. It was not until He appeared to all, and reprimanded them for their disbelief, that they finally realized it was true. Are we so different? How often has God worked in our lives to fulfill the dream or answer a prayer, and yet each time we need help we do not quite believe-this time-He will answer.

Jesus taught life is for living. Abundant life is lived from within. Thoughts held in mind create after their kind. That which you <u>truly</u> believe, shall come to pass. He walked the same path we do today. He overcame the world's temptations and asked us to 'follow Him'. He blazed the trail for us. Jesus the Christ will complete His mission when <u>we</u> realize we are His siblings; therefore, One with Him-One with God-One with each other.

Christ the Lord is risen today. He is alive and lives in each of us. Look at Easter as your demonstration of divinity. Roll away the stone of limitation; know thyself! <u>You</u> are the Only Begotten Son of God!

"For God so loved the world, that He gave his only begotten Son, (the Christ within) that whosoever believeth in Him should not perish, but have everlasting life" (John 3:16)

God bless you, you beautiful expressions of God.

ADDENDUM

It was my intention to end at this point; however, during the writing of the book, a show aired on television, called *Revelations,* and I felt drawn to alleviate some fears concerning this work. For too long, too many view the Book of Revelations as a book of doom and gloom. One hears from many fearful people, "the end of the world is coming," "just look at the signs-prophesies are being fulfilled." I well understand many religions teach this, and believe it, to be true. I certainly am not attempting to disparage anyone's religion. We follow what is in our heart, and our inner guide, if this has been and continues to be your belief, so be it. If you are one of the many who are confused, fearful, and do not understand the Book of Revelations, may the following give you further insight.

Revelations-written by John, who was the most beloved and the youngest disciple of Jesus. He represents the Power of love. This alone should give one pause because Love, true Love, could not envision such dire and dreaded prophesies as <u>literally</u> written. John, being the youngest, had not had time to become hardened to life, and I believe he was optimistic about Jesus and His teachings.

Jesus spoke in parables to confuse His enemies. That is what is meant by "*He that hath ears to hear, let them hear.* (Matthew 11:15) Those who were open to God's Truth would listen and understand while those who were not would walk away bewildered. John wrote metaphysically, he 'saw' his visions from a higher state of consciousness. In order for us to understand, we too must 'see' from a higher consciousness. Therefore, I have included one more message-giving the metaphysical interpretation of the Four Horsemen-found in chapter 6 of Revelations.

Ride The White Horse

Good Morning!

My first thought, for today's message, was to speak about love. When it comes to making important decisions, I go on instinct, and nothing significant leaped out at me. Then by accident, if there is such a thing, I thought about the book of Revelations, and the many fears surrounding it. I decided, instead of speaking about love directly, I would give you a gift of love by presenting to you a message I prayerfully hope will alleviate some fears, and give you a better understanding of that dreaded last book of the Bible.

The Book of Revelation is the least understood book in the Bible. It deals <u>wholly</u> with states of consciousness, and as with the rest of the Bible should not be taken literally. John, the author of Revelations, deliberately disguised the writings so those who would read them would make a conscious effort to discover the spiritual significance of his visions. In other words he was telling the readers, "if you want to know the Truth, delve more deeply into what I am saying, listen, really listen, hear the meaning of my words."

He wrote the book in apocalyptic form, which means symbolic imagery. This was the type of writing greatly used among the Jewish people in the second century BC, and it extended into the Christian era. The times were dangerous, and so it was necessary for writers to use the symbolism that the people would understand. For example, they knew that Babylon meant Rome, and the Lamb represented the Christ.

Seekers of Truth do not limit the interpretation of Revelations as predictions of historical events. They were aware that John had a two-fold purpose. The <u>first</u> was to give <u>assurance</u> to all Christians that God is All-powerful, and saves everyone; that Spirit is stronger and more powerful than any "evil" force. The <u>second</u> was to furnish a chart, a map for Spiritual enfoldment, a path to the Christ within, and to provide an account of one's journey, from the first moment of his/her awakening to the glorious realization of one's Divinity. Jesus proved the Divinity in man; Revelations confirms it!

Today, we will examine the Four Horsemen of the Apocalypse. These horsemen represent <u>the key to the nature of man.</u> Once one understands this, then one can achieve dominion over self. Let me repeat, contrary to widespread belief, <u>the Bible does not predict</u> outcome. If it did, we would not have free will, nor would there be a need for prayer. Why pray if the conclusion is inevitable, if the plan for our future certain? However, we <u>can</u> change the future through our prayers, actions, and attitudes.

The Four Horsemen represent the four elements in human nature, physical, emotional, intellectual, and Spiritual. We know from studying "Truth" that the day will come when the first three natures will blend, giving way to Spirit, and then we will be free to state we are Spiritual Beings!"

I will begin with the Pale horse.

"...and his name that sat upon him was Death, and Hell followed with him..." (6:8)

Pale is the color of fright. When we are frightened, our skin turns an ashen gray. The pale horse is the first nature we are concerned with, the physical body. This scripture tells us anyone who rides on him is doomed and hell follows. If one lives <u>just</u> for the body, it will bring destruction on this plane. Concentrating solely on the body, eventually one begins to fear the thought of illness and growing old. Then as one sees the signs of age, the wrinkles appear, strands of gray hair, maybe developing some aches and pains, the fear begins to manifest. There is a feeling of frustration and emptiness. The apprehension increases and we are consumed with "What is ahead of me?" Ergo, "Hell follows after." Hell is a state of consciousness where one is <u>not</u> in peace. Living just for the body means giving the body power over the mind instead of recognizing <u>Mind is the Maker</u>, and therefore, more powerful than the body. The pale horse also stands for the material things in life. When we put money, and what it can do for us, first, then we are astride the pale horse. If money is one's god, he may amass it, but his life will be a living hell. Scrooge, in Charles Dickens *A Christmas Carol*, is a perfect example of this. Of course, to live on the human plane, we all need money. The mistake is putting it above God. Money will not give anyone continued peace of mind; it will not buy one wholeness, or help one achieve a Spiritual life. Only faith in God, can give us these. Other riders of the pale horse are those who want only prestige and standing in a community, no matter what the cost. They care not for the good they do, but for the reputation, it serves them.

"And there went out another horse that was Red: and power was given to him that sat thereon to take peace from the earth, and that they should kill one another: and there was given unto him a great sword." (6:4)

The red horse is your emotional nature. It can be just as dangerous to let our emotions take control as to allow the body full sway. The red horse is just as corrupt and can disrupt more lives.

To digress a moment, I have heard people say, "Do not listen to your feelings but rely on facts." I say this is only half-right. When someone experiences a severe challenge, finds himself in a disturbing relationship, or an illegal situation, it is because he/she was 'feeling with the senses (in other words using the body, "it feels good"). However, when one is using their instinct or intuition, which is "the still small voice within," that also appears as a feeling, and those are the feelings we should heed. Listening to the feelings that the body controls, such as, "I want, I must have," is allowing the emotions to take complete control.

Uncontrolled emotions can wreck us. There is a way to know the difference between sense feeling and Spiritual. If what you are doing is exclusively for you, if it is purely a selfish act, then it is coming from the ego (senses). However, if it is for the good of all concerned, a loving and unselfish act, that is from Spirit.

We are cautioned not to talk about religion or politics because these are two topics, which will raise uncontrolled emotions. I venture to guess there are those who have never studied the doctrine of their church, but will resent any critique, and argue when they do not have any facts. There are those who do not know the principle behind their political party, but will argue until blue in the face to justify a point. On the other hand, too little emotion is just as bad. These people are very nice but they never are noticed, and they drift through life without any feeling. The elder son in "The Prodigal Son" was a dutiful son. He did what he was told, but resented his brother, who listened to his feelings as controlled by the body, but later "came to himself". He listened to his intuition, and followed his creative instinct. Strong emotion is good, it is a power, which will bring you through a crisis, or carry you to a mountaintop *if* you stay in control.

Here is a little quiz to let you know if you are riding the red horse.

Do you ever get angry when contradicted?

Do you ever 'fly off the handle' over nothing?

Do you try to run the lives of, or interfere with, the way your family members live?

Think about it, each of us has our own internal guide, voice, or angel, to show us right from wrong, and we have free choice to listen or not. Do we really have the right, or should we take the time away from our own Spiritual development to impress on anyone, 'we are right or know it all'? If we truly believe in the Spirit within-should we not allow that Spirit to direct others too?

> *"And I beheld, and lo a Black horse; and he that sat on him had a pair of balances in his hand. And I heard a voice in the midst of the four beasts say, A measure of wheat for a penny, and three measures of barley for a penny;..."* (V: 5-6)

The black horse is the intellect. I am sure, in the course of your lifetime, you have come across some brainy types. When I was a teenager, if you were not going, or had not attended a college, you were considered a 'poor relation' by those who did. I do not believe it is so today. The television show, *The Apprentice,* proved that when Donald Trump pitted the Street Smarts with the College Graduates. The book learners who rely on facts <u>only</u>, are the intellectuals referred to in Revelations, and are most definitely riding the black horse.

There are those who believe that you can learn all there is to know about God, and the Universe from books. They form groups and discuss philosophy, theology, the pros and cons, and the why's and wherefores of meditation. They discuss and discuss, go deeper and deeper into intellectual analysis, and get nowhere. The intellect alone does not give answers. Spinoza said, "To define God is to deny Him."

The intellect will say, "There is no life after death because one can not take the body with him." (You see, to the intellect the body is everything because you can touch, see and feel with it). However, we who <u>know</u> are aware that

Life is Eternal; life continues on, in or out of the body. Some will say the brain thinks; therefore, when the brain rots in the grave, the thinker no longer exists. The mind thinks, not the brain; the mind resides in every cell of the body, and if the brain is removed from the body, <u>it</u> stops thinking, because it has been separated from the creative force of the mind. The intellectuals cannot believe in prayer because they cannot prove prayer changes things, but we who have had prayers answered, know and believe.

Those who ride the black horse have no knowledge of Spiritual understanding. They do not know to seek God is to find him, because finding him is done through the feeling nature. Without this "knowledge", they eventually become depressed, disappointed, and frustrated, for they depend entirely on the human aspect, only to discover man is undependable.

"And I saw, and behold a White horse: and he that sat on him had a bow; and a crown was given unto him: and he went forth conquering, and to conquer. (6:2)

The white horse is man's Spiritual nature; our real eternal self; the 'I AM' of us. This is our rightful inheritance, the <u>acceptance</u> that we are one with God and all humankind, the realization that we can say, as our brother did, "*I and the Father are one*". It gives us the awareness that all that the Father has, joy, abundance, harmony and happiness, is ours by Divine Right. The white horse is the realization of the Presence of God, the awareness of Oneness through the Christ within. Those who ride the white horse put God <u>first</u> in all ways and in all things. They do not limit God. They trust Him explicitly, and gallop to freedom from want, disease and poverty.

The horseman has a bow, an ancient symbol for the spoken word. One speaks the word, and it goes forth straight as an arrow, and does not come back void. The word, whether silent or audible, goes forth with the same power and results.

The rider wears a crown, the symbol for victory. Working on one's Spiritual life through prayer and meditation, working through a challenge, and "putting God in charge", earns one a crown. He sits astride the white horse knowing his true identity; he speaks the word, and rides through life victorious.

I have faith that each of you here this morning is mounting the white horse. You are here because you desire peace of mind, healing, and happiness. The realization of "Christ within" is a breathtaking experience. To know, <u>really</u> know, "I am the very child of God. Christ lives in me. The Father and I are One, We are One" frees us from all human pitfalls of jealousy, resentment, unforgiveness, and the like.

"What is man, that thou art mindful of him? And the son of man, that thou visitest him? For thou hast made him a little lower that the angels, and hast crowned him with glory and honor. Thou madest him to have dominion over the works of thy hands: thou hast put all things under his feet:" (Psalms 8:4-6)

Every man, woman, and child is His means of expression. When you look up here at me, you see the Father, for He walks and talks through me. Looking out at you this morning, I see the Father, for he walks and talks through you. He is ever with us. There is nothing created more powerful than each one of us. He has given us perfection, and dominion over <u>all</u> things; all things that we are <u>willing to accept,</u> and understand. That is the key. If you have a doubt, even a slim doubt, you must recognize it. Realize, what <u>you</u> are willing to accept <u>is</u> yours by Divine Right. This was/is Jesus' message. He came to teach. He came to prove the Truth. He stated, *"Think not that I have come to destroy the law, or the prophets: I am not come to destroy, but to fulfill."* (Matthew 5:17) He came to show us there is only One Power and One Presence, and It is good. That Power is Love.

I began this morning saying this was not primarily a message on love, but I was wrong. Love is the cohesive power that heals all, recognizes all, and accepts all. Love is the Spiritual link that makes us one.

I give you a challenge today, I ask that you make a commitment to yourself to use God's Love, physically, by reaching out to someone in need; emotionally, by feeling, deep within, "I need not be afraid of anyone or anything for God is in charge of my life;" and Spiritually, by knowing " The Father and I are one".

The horses are ready for you to ride: pale, red, black, and white. Mount the white horse and ride straight through the gates of heaven.

God bless you! I truly love you. I behold the Christ in you!

EPILOGUE

Well friends, we have come to the end of this journey. The messages within were written over a course of many years and there may be some repetition due to the nature of each talk It is my hope you have found some thought-provoking ideas to contemplate. You may have found some that you can easily agree with, and some that may sound ridiculous, even outlandish. As I said in the beginning, that is fine. As individuals, we have to follow what we firmly believe in, listen to our own inner guide, and come to conclusions that feel right. My intention was not to confuse, shock, or convert, but to open possibilities of 'what may be'. We live in a time where there seems to be so many questions of "Why?" and if we can understand that <u>Life is Consciousness,</u> and <u>Karma is Law,</u> it helps to soften the 'whys'.

Knowing that we have been given 'free will' to choose the course of our lives, even the coming in, and going out, (birth and death) gives answers to perplexing questions. The main thing to remember is <u>all choices take place in the subconscious.</u> Consciously, a person will say he/she does not want to be sick, but the dread of an important meeting, or event, and the wish not to be a part of it, will activate the subconscious to fulfill the desire. This is nothing to fear, only things to become aware of. Making the correct choices in life not only answers questions, but also opens the way to the fulfillment of an abundant life.

I truly bless you as you make this adventurous journey on the earth plane. I have enjoyed traveling along this stretch of road with you.

I leave you with Unity's *Prayer of Protection*

> The Light of God surrounds you;
> The Love of God enfolds you;
> The Power of God protects you;
> The Presence of God watches over you;
> WHEREVER YOU ARE, GOD IS!

ABOUT THE AUTHOR

Joanne has been a student of Truth her entire life and has worked as a Unity minister since 1978. In 1980, she founded Christ Unity in Panama City, Florida. She has served in ministries in Florida, Tennessee, Georgia, and Indiana in her career as a Unity minister and teacher. She feels that research, study, and meditation, have led her to discover the "power to create" in her life, which has led to a deeper understanding of life's joys and tragedies.

Joanne is a mother of three and grandmother of five. Although retired, she continues to teach and speak sharing her insights and wisdom.

Printed in the United States
134415LV00003B/7/P